THE DALES WAY

COLIN SPEAKMAN

1995

Dalesman Publishing Company

Stable Courtyard, Broughton Hall,
Skipton, North Yorkshire BD23 3AE

First edition 1970
Eighth edition 1995

Text © Colin Speakman 1995
Photographs © Geoff Lund 1995

Cover: Appletreewick and Simon's Seat by Geoff Lund

A British Library Cataloguing in Publication record
is available for this book
ISBN 1 85568 072 6

Printed by Lavenham Press   ·
Typeset by Lands Services

CONTENTS

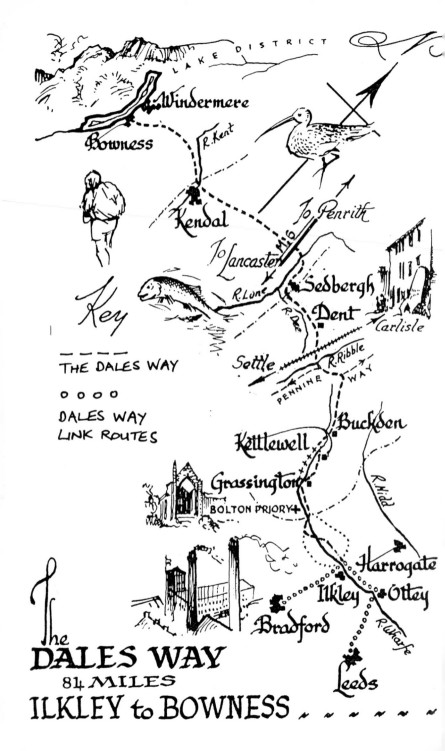

Windermere

Bowness

LAKE DISTRICT

R. Kent

Kendal

To Penrith

M6

To Lancaster

R. Lune

R. Dee

Sedbergh

Dent

Carlisle

Settle

R. Ribble

PENNINE WAY

Key

THE DALES WAY

DALES WAY
LINK ROUTES

Buckden

Kettlewell

Grassington

BOLTON PRIORY ✝

R. Nidd

Harrogate

Ilkley

Otley

R. Wharfe

Bradford

Leeds

The
DALES WAY
84 MILES
ILKLEY to BOWNESS

1. INTRODUCTION

The 135 km (84 mile) Dales Way between Ilkley to Bowness-on-Windermere is one of Britain's longest established and best loved Long Distance Footpaths. It was devised by Tom Willock and Colin Speakman, members of the West Riding Area of the Ramblers' Association in 1968, as a way of enjoying a continuous riverside walk, using existing rights-of-way and permissive paths along three of the most beautiful rivers in the Yorkshire Dales – the Wharfe, the Dee and the Lune.

But having taken the route close to the old Westmorland boundary at Crook of Lune, in the Lune Gorge, at the northwest boundary of the Yorkshire Dales National Park, rather than end the walk in a remote corner of the Dales, it seemed logical to link into a second National Park, the Lake District, by taking a route which crossed through the gentle green foothills of Southern Lakeland and partly following the banks of the rivers Mint, Spring and Kent to reach the shores of England's grandest and most famous lake, Windermere. The route was approved in principle by the old West Riding and Westmorland County Councils.

The first complete walk along the Dales Way following this initial research was undertaken by a Venture Scouts Unit from Bradford Grammar School in atrocious weather during the early spring of 1969. Fleur and Colin Speakman then surveyed the full route in detail in the summer of 1969, and the route was first described and published by Colin Speakman in the first edition of this guidebook by the Dalesman Publishing Company in 1970.

Since its inception more than a quarter of a century ago, the Dales Way has become one of Britain's most popular long distance routes. It has been officially recognised as a Recreational Footpath, and even though the route as such has never been formally approved, it appears on Ordnance Survey Maps. The Dales Way is now on a short list for consideration by the Countryside Commission for full National Trail status. Interestingly enough, requests for information by users have indicated that the Dales Way is already more popular among walkers than many of the official National Trails.

The prime reason for this popularity is the beauty and the variety of the landscape through which the Dales Way passes, from rich, fertile wooded valley scenery in central Wharfedale or along the Lune, to the rugged daleheads where the same rivers are little more than sparkling mountain streams, and open moorland where the path crosses the Pennine watersheds. Though it is essentially a low level route – for the record, one of the first such in Britain – as its name implies taking advantage of natural passes formed by steep, often glacier-carved river valleys through the

Central Pennines, it does have some dramatic high level sections, most notably above the watershed of the Wharfe and the Dee on Cam Fell, and along magnificent high level limestone pastures and terraces high above the river in Upper Wharfedale.

Another reason for the popularity of the Dales Way is its accessibility. From the very beginning the Dales Way was conceived as a route people of all ages and walking abilities would want to walk, so it doesn't lose itself in remote and hostile places away from human civilisation and creature comforts. It takes in a number of welcoming villages with a choice of pubs, shops, bed and breakfast accommodation in village inns or wayside cottages, as well as youth hostels. There's also good farmhouse accommodation to be found along much of the Way and in recent years, the addition of specially adapted Camping Barns, which are traditional barns converted to provide clean but basic self-catering accommodation for walkers usually close to the farmhouse.

Most of the walking is relatively easy, making it a suitable walk at least for older children in a family, though there are some more strenuous and tiring stretches in the central part of the route between Buckden and Dent, and a long stretch of countryside with few services between Sedbergh and Burneside.

Riverside walks are always especially rich in interest and the Dales Way is no exception. Sharing the company of a river from maturity to source is a special pleasure enjoyed by the Dales Way walker. Flowing water always has a fascination – deep and dark in the lower part of the dale, whisky brown higher up as it drains from high peaty moorland, flowing swiftly over water-smoothed pebbles. Within a couple hundred metres a still and tranquil river, mirroring banks and even hill tops in its placid surface, can change to a torrent of wild, white water rapids and cataracts. Yet another feature is the huge variety of fine, arched stone bridges, many of them centuries old, that carry lanes and roads over the river; all add to the delights of riverside walking.

The wildlife is fascinating in any season. The river banks in both the Dales and the Lake District are abundant in wildflowers in Spring – butterbur, celandines, primroses, campions, rock roses, kingcups, herb robert, violets. There's rarely a stretch without some birdlife – coot, mallard, heron and a variety of waders with even the occasional flash of a kingfisher in the lower reaches, dippers darting from rocks in the more mountainous stretches, as well as lapwing, curlew, skylark and kestrel on the high pastures and across open moorlands. The Wharfe is also a fine trout river; the gymnastic leaps made by trout after skimming flies can be an impressive sight and sound on a lazy summer's afternoon; salmon are to sometimes to be seen in the brown, swiftflowing waters of the Lune.

But the Dales Way is also a walk equally rich in history and legend. This is a landscape in which a medieval inheritance is clearly apparent, and seems always close – the monks who built the first bridges, the Plantagenent Forests where princes and bishops hunted wild boar and red deer, leaving scatterings of remnant woodlands in the gills and hunting lodges as lonely ruins; the isolated farmsteads whose names evoke their first Viking settlers, the old manorial mills still standing beside the rivers and becks that once turned their great wheels to grind villagers' corn.

Whatever season of the year, and indeed whatever the weather, the Dales Way is a rewarding experience. The short days of winter, with less visitors about, enjoy a special quality of light, and lack of leaf cover opens up vistas hidden in leafy summer days. Spring brings the wildflowers, the lambs, the pale green colours of new leaves. Summer is rich and lush, with longer days and brilliant light, whilst autumn, perhaps the most attractive of all the seasons, has glorious colours, rich scents and smells, and cooler days which are perfect for rambling.

One thing is certain, the Dales Way isn't a route to be rushed. It isn't a challenge walk, it isn't a marathon, and there are no prizes for anyone daft enough to do it within a certain time. This is a walk to take at a civilised, perhaps even a gentle pace, to savour over several days. It's a perfect short holiday, an opportunity to enjoy the countryside in ways which are only truly understood by the long distance walker, recapturing the sheer scale and grandeur of the landscape. This is something so easily reduced, and trivialised, by mechanised transport, especially the private car, which for all its convenience allows one of England's greatest landscapes to flicker past the windscreen in a matter of a couple of hours.

The Dales Way is all about rediscovering that subtlety, that complexity, that richness which is the Yorkshire Dales. It's a beauty which has to be enjoyed by all the senses, and not just by what is to be seen – the feel of the wind against your face, the sound of birdsong or a beck in spate, the scent of rotting leaves or cool, fresh earth, the taste of rain.

If it's the first time you've walked the Dales Way, you're someone to be envied.

2. PRACTICAL POINTS

The route

There is still no "official" Dales Way as such. This guidebook follows the original route as devised by the West Riding Ramblers in 1968/9, with a number of modifications resulting either from footpath creations or diversion orders, together with a deviation, between Addingham and Bolton Bridge, essential in terms of road safety.

Estimates of distances have in the past caused some confusion. Our original 1968 survey indicated a route of some 73 miles but later commentators have suggested first 81 and more recently Paul Hammon's detailed guide in his *Dales Way Companion* suggests 84 miles (135 km), a figure which reflects careful research and which for this book I now accept as accurate – perhaps in those early days our map measures showed slightly longer Yorkshire rather than standard Imperial miles!

Most Dales Way walkers follow the route from south to north, if for no other reason than Ilkley, on the edge of the West Yorkshire conurbation, is so easy to reach by public transport and yet signifies the point where the true Dales country begins. The Lake District is also an inspiring destination for any walker heading away from the West Yorkshire centres of industry and population towards the romantic landscapes of the Lake District.

Another point to bear in mind is that the prevailing wind comes from the southwest. This means there's less chance of a headwind if you're walking northwestwards. It's also easier to walk with the sun in the south behind you rather than in your eyes.

But it is perfectly possible to walk the Dales Way in the reverse direction, from Bowness to Ilkley, and quite a few people do, though a guidebook has yet to be written with a north-south orientation.

How to use this book

The Dales Way isn't a difficult route to find. However, this guidebook is intended to be a compact guide to help route finding, not to replace accurate map reading. Good maps are essential.

At time of writing, there is still no consistent waymark symbol in use along the Dales Way (though one is currently being planned by the Dales Way Association and may well appear during the life of this guidebook). The name Dales Way will, however, be seen on quite a large number of wooden footpath signs, though there is a tendency in the Yorkshire Dales National Park to indicate the next destination along the route without including the name Dales Way.

Most of the Dales Way is well signposted where it leaves metalled roads, though waymarking is only sporadic – perhaps better in the Lake District than the Yorkshire Dales. Whilst this is no problem in the heavily used sections of Wharfedale where the path is clearly visible on the ground, north from Dentdale the path is far less obvious and considerable care is still required, either using the appropriate excellent 1:25,000 Outdoor Leisure and Pathfinder Maps (see the recommended list at the end of this chapter) or at least 1:50,000 Landrangers together with the detailed sketch maps by Arthur Gemmell for Stile Maps or Paul Hannon in his *Dales Way Companion*.

The Stile Maps booklet also shows a number of circular walks or attractive deviations that can be made using sections of the Dales Way to or from a parked car without having to retrace one's steps back along the Dales Way.

The Leeds and Bradford Links

Stile Maps also feature the Ramblers' Association's recommended Dales Way Link Routes both from and to Bradford and Leeds.

The Bradford Link (15km – 9 miles) starts at Shipley, on the outskirts of Bradford, going via historic Saltaire, Shipley Glen and Dick Hudson's before taking the paved packhorse-way across Ilkley Moor, before descending past White Wells to join the main Dales Way at Ilkley Bridge.

The Leeds Link (17 km – 17 miles) follows a winding green corridor from Woodhouse Moor near the city centre, and snakes its way by remarkably rural, mainly wooded footpaths out of the city via the Meanwood Valley, Adel Woods, Eccup, Bramhope and Otley Chevin before following the edge of Burley and Ilkley Moors to Ilkley.

A Harrogate Link has also been suggested from Harrogate to Bolton Abbey via Upper Washburndale, but no route has so far been finalised.

Public transport and accommodation

The Dales Way is extremely well served at either end by public transport, with buses and trains to and from both Ilkley and Bowness/Windermere. This makes it possible to plan the entire walk without having to use a car, thus reducing the need to leave a parked car as a temptation for thieves, or indeed adding to traffic congestion and pollution in the countryside.

Frequent soon-to-be electrified trains to and from Leeds and

Bradford link with Inter-City and Regional Railway services and operate half hourly (Sundays hourly) to the start of the route at Ilkley. There are also buses from Leeds, Bradford, Otley, Keighley and Skipton. Returning from Bowness, local buses shuttle to Windermere where The Lakes branch line feeds into Inter-City services at Oxenholme. Local buses and express coaches serve Kendal, Lancaster and other parts of England.

But the Dales Way is also a route which can be walked in day or weekend stages without having to use a car, or by using combination of car and public transport thanks to excellent intermediate bus and train services, without all the extra pollution and disturbance resulting from two drivers and two cars – a very environmentally damaging way of walking a long distance trail. Inevitably planning is, however, necessary in the remoter areas, though use of the Upper Wharfedale school bus from Buckden and Kettlewell (weekdays) and the Dalesbus (summer weekends) provide invaluable return transport both for park-and-ride walkers and those who rely totally on public transport.

The central parts of the Dales Way are now splendidly served by the recently reopened stations at Ribblehead and Dent on the scenic Settle-Carlisle railway. Sedbergh is a little more problematic, though a limited local service and taxis link to Kendal and Oxenholme stations exists.

In the Lake District stations at Burneside and Staveley on the Windermere branch are strategically placed, supplemented by frequent bus services into Kendal.

This book has therefore been planned to utilise day stages which reflect available transport and accommodation provision.

Details of public transport including local taxi firms are contained in the Dales Way Handbook, free to all members of the Dales Way Association or £1.20 post free from the Association's Secretary, David Smith, Dalegarth, Moorfield Road, Ilkley, West Yorkshire, LS29 7NA.

Detailed public transport timetables for the Yorkshire Dales – including buses serving most of the Dales Way from Ilkley to Sedbergh as well as trains from Ribblehead and Dent – are also contained in *Dales Connections* available from National Park Centres and local Tourist Information Centres by sending 60p in stamps to Elmtree Press & Distribution, The Elms, Exelby, Bedale, North Yorkshire, DL8 2HD.

The Dales Way Handbook also contains a regularly revised and updated accommodation guide.

There is an excellent choice of accommodation on the Dales Way, ranging from bunk house to small country house hotels. Camping is, however, more limited, though there are official sites in the Appletreewick and Dentdale areas. There are youth hostels at Linton (near Grassington) Kettlewell, Denthead, and Kendal.

Clothing and equipment

Though the Dales Way is not a mountain route, it has some extremely exposed upland sections. At any time of the year, good protective clothing is essential – a windprooof anorak, rainwear – including overtrousers – a spare sweater, and a decent pair of boots. Modern lightweight boots are perfectly adequate – the terrain can be muddy and wet, but is not tough.

Carry a small first aid kit, and – for emergencies – a "bivvy bag" which can be supplied by any outdoor shop at modest cost. Emergency food and drink is also essential, and a compass is useful even though there are few points when the Dales Way walker is far from friendly landmarks.

Recommended maps

Landranger – Sheets 97, 98, 104.

Outdoor Leisure: Sheets 2 Yorkshire Dales Western Area, 7 Lake District South Eastern Area; 10 Yorkshire Dales Southern Area; 30 Yorkshire Dales (Northern and Central Areas) plus *Pathfinder* Sheets 671 and 662 cover the section in West Yorkshire between Ilkley and Bolton Bridge, whilst Sheet 617 which covers the narrow gap in South Lakeland that lies between the Dales and Lakeland Outdoor Leisure maps.

The Dales Way Route Guide – Arthur Gemell and Colin Speakman (Stile Maps, Otley) – this contains detailed maps of the entire route with circular link walks plus the Leeds and Bradford Link Paths.

The Dales Way Companion Paul Hannon (Hillside Publications, Keighley). This attractively produced handbook contains detailed Wainwright-style maps and delightful line drawings of features along the entire route.

3. THE DALES WAY ASSOCIATION

Over the quarter of a century that the Dales Way has been in being, progress towards official recognition of the route has been slow.

We imagined in 1968 that short sections of "missing" path where road walking is required, such as between Beckermonds and Oughtershaw in Langstrothdale, or in Upper Dentdale, would eventually be filled by Footpath Creation Agreements, a mechanism through which landowners would receive generous compensation for granting a right of passage across his or her land to take walkers off the road. What we failed to understand then that the continuing lack of generosity by some landowners in granting access to their land, together with the feebleness of local authorities in securing footpath agreements would force walkers to remain on dangerous, heel-hurting tarmac. It's actually far, far easier in Britain to build a kilometre of six lane motorway through the countryside than it is to create a 100 metre length of metre-wide riverside footpath.

The one notable exception was at Fairfield, north of Addingham where the negotiating skill of Tom Willcock, at that time Footpath Secretary of the West Riding Ramblers' Association, the far sightedness of a landowner and the refreshing energy of the local authority, Bradford City Council, secured a beautiful section of riverside path between Fairfield House and Lobwood House for the Dales Way with a Footpath Creation Agremeent – so far the only one to have been achieved on the Dales Way.

But progress on waymarking has been equally disappointing. Despite discussions over an official waymark and logo with the Countryside Commission in the 1970s, no logo was agreed. Signing and waymarking of the route remain extremely inconsistent, with no common, recognisable waymark. In places maintenance, too, is inadequate for a route of this nature, with wobbly stiles and poor surfaces. Ironically, some of the least well waymarked sections lie within the Yorkshire Dales National Park despite some excellent maintenance in other sections, where, incidentally, the overwhelming usage is by visitors taking short, circular walks from heavily-used Wharfedale car parks rather than Dales Way long distance walkers as such.

Lack of progress on recognising the Dales Way and providing a consistent system of waymarking throughout its length has led to frustration and a feeling among ramblers that an organisation was needed to bring together both users and providers along the Dales Way. So the Dales Way Association represents both walkers and tourist organisations who fully understand the value of "green" or sustainable forms of tourism in the countryside as represented by the Dales Way, reflecting both conservation values and the economic benefit of sustainable forms of tourism in the rural community. Another aim, too, is to secure considerate behaviour from users of the route towards farmers and landowners and to ensure dialogue with farmers to help reduce any problems caused by the route across their land.

So early in 1992, with the active support of the Ramblers' Association Lakeland and West Riding Areas and also of the South Lakeland Tourist Association, the Dales Way Association was born.

Objectives of the Association are as follows:

1. To consider the route and status of the Dales Way Long Distance Footpath Route and related footpath links, and to support their appropriate maintenance, signing and waymarking.

2. To encourage the interpretation and conservation of the Dales Way and the landscape corridor through which it passes.

3. To take an active role in the marketing and promotion of the Dales Way in ways that help to retain its essential character.

4. To keep an up-to-date register of accommodation, route changes, transport and related facilities for the benefit of users of the Dales Way.

Anyone who has walked the route and who supports the Association's objectives (including readers of this guide) are invited to join the Association which already has well over a hundred members. A regular Newsletter is produced, and all members receive a copy of the Dales Way Handbook. The official logo – representing the Dales Way passing through a range of hills – has been adopted by the Association and is reproduced overleaf. This is now used for the official Dales Way badge and also for the Dales Way certificate.

The official Dales Way cloth rucksack badge can be obtained price £1.50 post free from the Association (address below) or from certain shops/TICs along the route, including the Lake District National Park Visitor Centre at Bowness.

The Dales Way certificate is available to anyone completing the route, on receipt of a report of their walk, which will include the full name of those participating, and date started and finished, and any other information or comments walkers would like to make. Certificates can be obtained from Frank Sanderson at a cost of £1.50 per certificate, (cheques payable to Frank Sanderson) Blenheim Lodge, Brantfell Road, Bowness on Windermere, Cumbria, LA23 3AE.

All Dales Way walkers are encouraged to submit reports and suggestions about the route itself, about accommodation provision, waymarking or any other aspect of interest. Problems on the route are best identified with a grid reference. These will be dealt with either directly by the Association's officers or passed onto the relevant authorities.

Regular detailed surveys of the route are undertaken by members of the Association, problems reported and their solution monitored. Recommendations for minor diversons of the route are also being discussed and progressed. In the longer term improvements to the route will be considered, including loops or links, especially where road walking is involved, and the Association will consider whether the Dales Way should, in future years, be proposed for full National Trail status, as its popularity and usage suggests it should.

Occasional events are organised for members, including the annual meeting which is usually combined with a short walk along part of the Dales Way.

The current (1994) fee for membership of the Association is a modest £4 per annum. The secretary of the Association is David Smith, Dalegarth, Moorfield Road, Ilkley, West Yorkshire, LS29 8BL; in case of difficulty letters to the Association may also be forwarded by the Dalesman Publishing Company.

the dales way

4. YORKSHIRE DALES AND LAKE DISTRICT NATIONAL PARKS

The Dales Way traverses the whole of Yorkshire Dales National Park in a south-east to north-west direction between Bolton Bridge in Wharfedale and Crook of Lune in Lonsdale, and after a short intermediate section between the rivers Lune and Kent, enters the Lake District National Park just north of Cowan Head between Burneside and Staveley.

National Parks represent the highest status of landscape designation in England and Wales. But the name can, at times, cause confusion; in the UK National Parks are neither "nationally" owned nor are they "parks" in the usually accepted sense of the word. They are areas of countryside designated as being of national importance for their special landscape qualities and recreational opportunities. This means in practice that land is mainly privately owned and that access is identical to anywhere else in Britain, that is along public rights of way, and across certain areas of open moorland or fellside above enclosed farmland where there are formal access agreements or, as in much of the Lake District or parts of the Yorkshire Dales, there is a long tradition of tolerated or "de facto" access. Additional government funding ensures higher standards of planning and development control, as well as more facilities for interpretation and visitor management.

The Yorkshire Dales National Park, the third largest of the eleven National Parks is noted above all for its dramatic limestone scenery, a landscape dominated by high scars, crags, caves, limestone pavements and long terraces, but also for the contrast between the bare, treeless, sculptured shapes of the upland ridges and with the intimate beauty of the valleys with their fast flowing rivers, wooded gills, farms with scattered barns, intricate patterns of drystone walls, herb rich meadows, and unspoiled stone villages.

The Lake District National Park, the largest of the parks, is a landscape of even more ancient volcanic and sedimentary rocks, of higher, more jagged peaks including Scafell Pike at 978 metres England's highest summit, as well as the series of splendid lakes which gives the region its name. This is the landscape that inspired the greatest of England's Romantic poets and painters, Wordsworth, Coleridge, Southey, Girtin, Turner, Cotman, and many others. Whilst the Dales Way really explores only the less-frequented foothills of the Lakeland mountains, it provides a fitting prelude to the glorious landscapes of the central areas.

Both within and outside the National Park privacy should be respected. Treat those you meet and their land and property you cross with the courtesy which is due. Keep to rights of way across farmland, close gates unless they are clearly meant to be left open, always take all litter back home or back to your accommodation with you, and above all, if you have a dog keep it under firm control, preferably on a lead, at all times, and especially when crossing fields where there is stock. Problems can be acute at lambing time – between March and May. Nothing upsets farmers more than to see ill-behaved dogs at such times – please ensure that such things do not occur on the Dales Way. For Dales Way walkers there's a lot to be said for the American National Parks slogan – when walking in the countryside take only photographs and leave only footprints.

For fuller information about the Yorkshire Dales National Park contact the Yorkshire Dales National Park Information Services, Colvend, Hebden Road, Grassington, via Skipton, North Yorkshire, BD23 5LB tel 0756 752748. There are National Park Centres along the Dales Way at Grassington (in the main car park) and in Sedbergh (Joss Lane at the eastern end of the High Street).

For information about the Lake District National Park contact Brockhole National Park Centre, Windmere, Cumbria, LA23 1LJ tel 05394 46601. There is a National Park and Tourist Information Centre at Bowness, at the end of the Dales Way, close to the Lake foreshore.

Two active voluntary organisations concerned with the protection of the National Parks are the Yorkshire Dales Society, Civic Centre, Cross Green, Otley, West Yorkshire, LS21 1HD and the Friends of the Lake District, No 3, Yard 77, Highgate, Kendal, Cumbria, LA9 4ED.

MID-WHARFEDALE
ILKLEY to GRASSINGTON

17 miles (28 km)

Break points

Addingham   2.5 miles (4 km) – bus 783, 762/765
Bolton Abbey   6.5 miles (10 km) – bus 76, 800
Barden   9.5 miles (15 km) – bus 76, 800
Burnsall   13.5 miles (22 km) – bus 76, 800

This first 17-mile stage of the Dales Way might seem a long way to some people, but the walking is level and path finding fairly straightforward. The distance is easily covered by most experienced walkers if you start out from Ilkley early in the day. Grassington is an excellent accommodation base, with a choice of small hotels, inns and bed and breakfast establishments, Linton Youth Hostel is less than a mile away from the Dales Way at Linton Falls.

This section can be easily shortened by stopping at an intermediate point such as Barden or Burnsall, or by using either the (summer) weekends only late afternoon Dalesbus 800 back to Ilkley from Bolton Abbey, Barden or Burnsall, or the school bus 76 (not during school holidays) which will take you back to Skipton (connection on Yorkshire Rider 783 for Ilkley) or forward to Grassington at teatime.

The official start of the Dales Way is at Ilkley Bridge (SE 113482), not the present Edwardian Middleton Bridge carrying the main road to Middleton across the River Wharfe, but the narrow, hump-backed bridge dating from the 17th century, about 400 yards upstream through the riverside park. For many years this was the only bridge across the Wharfe between Otley and Bolton Bridge, a distance of some 12 miles. It is now closed to all but foot traffic and cycles.

Ilkley is a town with a long history. It was originally a Celtic settlement, Llecan, established within the federal kingdom of Brigantia, probably some time before Christ, and strategically sited by a shallow ford across the treacherous River Wharfe. After the Roman Conquest a small military fort guarding this same crossing was developed and it became a junction of important military roads that crossed the Aire/Wharfe Gap through the Pennines from Ribchester in Lancashire in the west and estwards to Tadcaster and York, as well as northwards through Wharfedale to Aldborough and Bainbridge in Wensleydale.

You can see the outline foundations of Olicana fort as a smooth flat-topped grassy mound immediately behind the medieval Parish church, whilst the little Tudor Manor House nearby contains many Roman and Romano British finds made in the area.

Warriors of a later age anglicised Olicana's name to Ilkley and left behind three ornately carved Anglo-Viking crosses, probably grave markers, which are kept inside the parish church.

But after centuries of being nothing but a quiet village, the discovery of the healing properties of an ice cold moorland spring on Ilkley Moor led to the growth of Ilkley as a spa town. At first travellers came on the new turnpike road from York, Boston Spa and the old market town of Otley. But by the mid 1860s when the railway lines were opened first from Leeds and then from Bradford, Ilkley became nationally known as "The Malvern of the North" or "The Heather Spa", famed for its water or hydropathic cures, its bracing moorland air – a contrast to smoke-filled Victorian towns – its comfortable hotels and guest houses, and elegant shopping parades which still survive to greet a new car as well as rail-served clientèle.

There is a good choice of accommodation and with its first class public transport links it makes an excellent starting point for a long distance walk.

A signpost by Ilkley Bridge confirms the start of the Dales Way on the south of the river by a small nursery. Take no notice of the 73 miles it is claimed to Bowness – this is characteristic Yorkshire understatement. The Dales Way begins along a riverside track behind gardens which soon join a drive to Ilkley Tennis Club and Sports Centre. Almost opposite the first of the larger Sports Centre buildings, a partly concealed kissing gate on the left (SE 107483) leads to a fairly clear path across low lying fields, heading to another kissing gate then alongside a fence, through another gate on the left, before keeping ahead through yet more gates and alongside hedge and fence to soon rejoin the riverside. Follow the riverside again, taking care along some wet and boggy land before the path narrows to a way between gardens and scrubby riverside trees, over a footbridge by a water inlet, continuing by the river before reaching a quiet lane which is in fact the old main road to Addingham before the first of several road widening and improvement schemes were completed, which now take the roar of the main A65 over the Addingham bypass.

The Dales Way follows this riverside lane, to a junction right, signed as the Dales Way (SE 090488) which takes the way along the access road into Addingham Low Mill village. This is an interesting adaptation of a former early Industrial Revolution textile mill complex with its attendant cottages which have been transformed into a Civic Trust award winning residential development. Weavers' cottages by the roaring mill race are now desirable designer homes, covered with roses and hanging baskets. It is

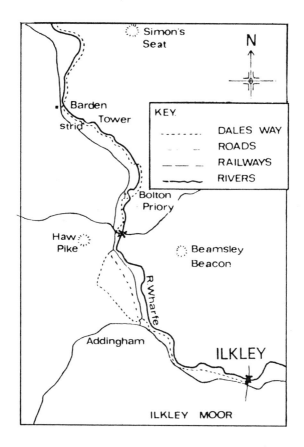

ironic to think that this mill was the scene of rebellious Luddite riots in 1829 when local handloom weavers, fearful for their skilled trade, smashed the new mechanised shearing frames.

A stile leads out of the cul-de-sac lane past the cottage terraces into another tarmac lane. Follow this for some 500 metres past the handsome gardens of the former vicarage to where a narrow path leads through a stile on the right and over a tiny hump-backed bridge. Ahead is Addingham's handsome 15th century church, with its blue-faced clock, dedicated to St. Peter. It was built around 1475, though much altered in the 18th and 19th centuries, its size reflecting the importance of this medieval settlement which expanded rapidly in the early years of the Industrial Revolution. It almost certainly replaced a much earlier church at "Long Addingham" as the settlement was known, where, according to legend, the Anglo-Saxon Christian Bishop Wulfere from York fled in 970 to hide from maurauding Danes. A thorn tree in the churchyard is reputed to be a cutting from the celebrated Christmas-flowering Glastonbury Thorn.

Turn left along the churchyard wall and follow the path over to another footbridge by cottages to Bark Lane.

Few Dales Way walkers probably bother to explore Addingham, which lies directly ahead. This is a pity because it's one of the most interesting early industrial townships in the Dales, with more buildings listed for architectural or historic interest than any other Dales village. Especially interesting are several very early mills where weavers' began sharing the same loft space to create a manufactory. There are no less than five pubs, including The Fleece, an 18th century coaching inn which still has most of its stables intact. These were used for changing horses before the stiff ascent over Chelker brow between Addingham and Skipton.

But the Dales Way continues to the right along Bark Lane where 250 metres to the right, just by the suspension bridge over the Wharfe (SE 083499) steps lead down to the riverside path – don't cross the bridge but keep to the left along the riverside.

You soon reach Addingham High Mill, another former water-powered textile mill which has been skilfully converted for residential use. Go past the mill and keep ahead directly through the caravan site before going through a gate on the right which leads back onto the riverbank. This path curves past the weir and over stiles to reach the busy B6160 road at a stile near Fairfield Hall. Almost immediately another stile on the right returns the Dales Way onto a lovely stretch of riverside path, dominated by the view of Beamsley Beacon across the river, a heather covered peak which forms a magnificent landmark and viewpoint, one of the great chain of beacons which crossed Northern England and brought news of the Spanish Armada in 1588.

Where this path once again reaches the road, to avoid an extremely dangerous stretch of narrow main road without a sidewalk (a stretch not recommended even though some maps and even some guidebook writers incorrectly suggest it is the Dales Way), the Dales Way walker must turn left for 50 metres to the entrance of Lob Wood House Farm (SE 077518), going along the track past the farm buildings and barn (which can be muddy) before following at track which crosses over a former railway line and bears right to a gate into a broad hillside pasture. The path ascends the pasture at 45 degrees to the left heading for the outside corner of a small wood to the right, 200 metres beyond which an intersecting path from the left descends to the field corner on the right – not visible on the ground. Turn right and head for the field corner where a slightly tricky stile leads into Lob Wood (SE 068523). The path turns sharp right in the wood before winding steeply down into the ravine (care needed – take your time) going along the slope of the hillside under the great arches of the former Midland Railway Line which ran from Ilkley to Skipton via Bolton Abbey and Embsay, a much lamented link closed in 1965 which may soon reopen between Embsay and Bolton Abbey as part of the Embsay Steam Railway. This path slopes down to the bottom of the wood – a fine place for bluebells – and curves to a gap stile in the wall which leads into the main B6160 road.

Cross with great care (the path leads directly into the line of very fast moving traffic) and turn left for 300 metres to where, just past a lay-by on the right, a stile leads over a footbridge to a path alongside the stream which goes underneath the new A59 flyover to emerge at the old Bolton Bridge.

In medieval times this was a ford with a small chantry where you said a prayer before crossing the dangerous river. Steps at the far side of the bridge lead down into a large field which, as a sign reminds you, forms part of the Chatsworth Estate at Bolton Abbey. The path crosses this wide field; following the fence before reaching the riverside as it curves from the right. The large expanse of pasture on the left between the river and the Devonshire Arms Hotel is reputed have been a cornfield where the brilliant Cavalier General, Prince Rupert, spent the night before his defeat at the hands of Cromwell's Ironsides in the Battle of Marston Moor, near York, in 1642.

For the next few miles pathfinding is easy. Bolton Priory is soon reached. The Priory gives its name to the village of Bolton Abbey and the two should not be confused. Here was a Priory of Augustinian Canons (Black Monks) who were given land by the Norman De Romilles of Skipton and came here from Embsay in 1154. Part of the original massive Priory Church is still in use as the parish church. The evocative ruins, superbly situated on a headland above a bend in the Wharfe, have long attracted poets, painters and writers – Wordsworth, Turner, Landseer and John Ruskin were among the most celebrated to be inspired by a special sense of place.

Few Dales Way walkers will want to miss an opportunity to enjoy the Priory; at weekends when services are not taking place guides are on duty to explain a little of the priory's remarkable history, including why Prior Moon's tower at the western end of the church was never completed until a roof was added in the 1980s. There is, of course, no charge for entry, but in common with other Dales churches, a small contribution to upkeep is always welcome – and ensure your boots are clean before going inside.

The hall opposite the priory was originally the monastic gatehouse but was transformed in the late 18th century into a neo-Gothic lodge which is still used by members of the Cavendish family and their guests when visiting Bolton. Though one the largest private estates in the Yorkshire Dales, the Chatsworth Estate has always freely welcomed visitors and shared the splendours of the grounds and woodlands. Until the 1960s thousands of day trippers came by train to Bolton Abbey station – in more recent times even greater numbers now come by car, using the village car park and the large informal car parks by the riverside.

The small and attractive village up the steps to the left has a post office, shop and excellent tea shops as well as a limited bus service.

The Dales Way crosses the Wharfe by the footbridge (stepping stones can be used by the intrepid if the river is low) and takes the path up the steps that leads to the right through Bolton Abbey Woods, soon bearing left with magnificent views back across the great bend in the river to the priory. These paths, were originally created by the Reverend William Carr, vicar of Bolton Abbey for the guests of the Duke of Devonshire in the 19th century. William Carr was a remarkable man; a considerable scholar in his own right he published the first dictionary of Yorkshire dialect and bred the celebrated Craven Heifer, a gigantic cow which still appears on local inn signs. The woods still form part of the extensive Chatsworth Estate and the paths have recently been improved and made easier to use. Most of the paths through the estate are not, at time of writing, public rights of way, and for this reason don't appear as such on OS maps, but they are available for use by walkers with the full permission of the Chatsworth Estate and form an integral part of the Dales Way.

The path eventually joins a narrow lane. Keep ahead to where the lane fords Pickles Gill (the footbridge to the right allows dry feet after rain) before going back to the riverside and taking a stile in the wall corner, leading to a riverside path. At the stile turn left over the wooden bridge to Cavendish Pavilion, a welcoming cafe and restaurant, together with toilets, which is open most days of the year.

Now follows one of the most romantically beautiful parts of the Dales Way through Strid Woods, a magnificent riverside walk rich in natural history and glorious views. The woods are mainly sycamore and beech with some oak, willow, ash, holly, alder and other species and the areas is noted for its variety of lichen, ferns, and fungi as well as birdlife – finches, woodpeckers, willow warblers. The well waymarked nature trails provide interesting variations to the main path. The paths converge at the terrifying Strid, a narrow sandstone chasm through which the entire force of the River Wharfe plunges, carving out deep underwater caverns. The name "Strid" is derived from "stride" and many of those who have attempted the deceptively difficult leap have paid with their lives, the most famous being the Boy of Egremond, heir to the great de Romille Estates in the 12th century. According to legend he was dragged back by his greyhound when leaping the Strid and like so many victims, was trapped under a rocky shelf until he drowned. A lifebelt is a grim and necessary reminder of the danger that is ever present, even when the river is low.

Recent erosion by rainwater has caused some problems on the

path that follows the steps through the crags, and it may be necessary to bear left uphill from the Strid – follow the yellow waymarks – to rejoin path which winds to the right by Pembroke Seat and out towards Barden, crossing the footbridge over Barden Beck, (SE 059567) and along the riverside. Keep ahead underneath the arch of the crenallated Edwardian aqueduct carrying waters of the Upper Nidderdale Reservoirs to Bradford, then through the woods behind Barden Tower before reaching the lovely, traditional stone bridge over the Wharfe at Barden.

Barden Tower, 250 metres up the hill along the lane to the left above Barden Bridge, is not to be missed. This was originally a hunting lodge built for the Cliffords, Lords of Craven in Plantagenent times. In 1461 when Butcher Clifford, the scourge of the Yorkists, was killed at the Battle of Towton in 1461, during the Wars of the Roses, legend relates that his widow, Margaret, placed her eldest son Henry to be raised in secret in the family of a Cumberland shepherd. Historians, though, have suggested that the child was more likely to have been hidden close to his mother's estate at Londsborough in the Yorkshire Wolds.

Years later, after Richard III perished at the Battle of Bosworth in 1485, the estates were restored to Henry Clifford, but the "Shepherd Lord" prefered living at Barden Tower rather than his great Castle in Skipton. Taught by the Canons of Bolton Priory, Clifford became a considerable scholar as well as a wise and just leader. In 1511, at almost 60 years of age, he fought for his King against the Scots at the Battle of Flodden.

The tower, now a preserved ruin, was restored by the last of the Cliffords, Lady Anne, Countess of Pembroke in 1659. Lady Anne was a remarkable woman who fought to regain and restore her ancestral estates after the Cromwellian period and who became a notable philanthropist. Her diaries, recently published, provide a remarkable record of life in 17th century Yorkshire. The plaque she placed on the wall of the ruined tower relates how her mother stayed there "bigge with child" and how she restored the building when she came into her estates.

The remarkable early Tudor Priest's House is now a tea room and restaurant. One of the farm buildings nearby has been converted into a bunkhouse barn for Dales Way walkers.

The route of the Dales Way between Barden and Grassington is easy to follow, along the north side of the river. From Barden Bridge a little stile leads to a narrow path alongside the inside wall by the lane – probably slightly safer than the often busy lane. This leads to a gentle riverside path, along the edge of fields, crossing stiles. This passes stepping stones at Drebley before curving into a track to the right along Fir Beck to Howgill Bridge (SE 593060).

The Dales Way crosses the bridge and returns over the far side of Fir Beck, over a stile and back to the riverside path over more

stiles and through a wooded gorge past a series of whitewater rapids. Soon the path emerges in more open country, passes campsites by the village of Appletreewick, a village once known for its onion fairs. This is another village worth a detour (service 76 bus weekdays – limited in school holidays). There are charming 16th and 17th century cottages, one of which is a fragment of a medieval grange, as well as two pubs.

Beyond the camp sites, another attractive section follows, this time the path traversing the gnarled roots of trees by the water's edge, before following the edge of fields through to Woodhouse Farm (SE 035040). Keep ahead through the farmyard, bearing slightly left past the farmhouse towards a footbridge, the easy to follow path ascending the embankment over stiles and heading across open pasture to the end of Burnsall Bridge. Turn left along the road to the village.

Burnsall is a jewel. It is a village in an almost perfect setting within a great bowl formed by heather and bracken covered fells. As well as the 17th century bridge with its massive breakwaters, there is a lovely medieval church with Viking "hog-backed" gravestones on display, a mullioned windowed Grammar school – still the village school – endowed in the 17th century by Sir William Craven, a local boy who left for London and like Dick Whittington, prospered to became Lord Mayor. For walkers with other needs there is a cafe, a village shop and a pub with real ale and rose covered walls.

The final part of the route to Grassington starts at the riverside between the car park and garden of the Red Lion Inn and the bridge, along a concreted stretch of path to resist river erosion,

Dales Way country. Bolton Abbey, looking down-dale towards Ilkley

The Strid, where the River Wharfe pounds through a mighty and terrifying chasm

Barden Bridge, a lovely example of traditional Dales architecture.

A superb drystone wall leads the eye updale from near Barden Bridge.

Sheep and lambs return to the fells at Hartlington, near Burnsall.

Bird's eye view of Burnsall from high on the nearby fell.

Leaves from spreading chestnut trees carpet the banks of the Wharfe near Hebden.

Grassington bridge, which has been successively enlarged over the centuries.

Abandoned farmstead at Barras, near the high-level stretch of the Dales Way from Grassington to Kettlewell.

Show day at Kilnsey as seen from the eastern slopes of Wharfedale

The sweeping roof of the modern church at ScarGill is a striking feature of Upper Wharfedale

Dramatic limestone outcrops looking south towards Kilnsey.

Kettlewell, once on the main coaching route from London to Richmond and the north. Great Whernside is in the background.

climbing a knoll to overlook a dramatic geological feature, Loup Scar, a limestone cliff above rocky rapids. This is the result of the great Mid-Craven Fault which crosses Wharfedale at this point. From Ilkley the predominant rock has been acid millstone grit, a form of coarse sandstone, and shale; north of Burnsall is the carboniferous or mountain limestone country of the Dales, creating a softer, gentler, lighter landscape with more fertile pastures, more wildflowers, and drystone walls which gleam grey white in sunlight – or silver in moonlight.

The Dales Way crosses this low limestone headland before returning to the riverside along another newly constructed stretch of path. At Hebden the river is crossed by an elegant little suspension bridge, originally built by a local blacksmith last century to replace still visible stepping stones, and was recently restored. It swings gently as you cross.

The Dales Way now bears left and follows a gentle section of riverside, the river now calm, shallow and broad, the path following an avenue of chestnut trees, richly colourful in spring and thick with conkers in autumn, going over stiles to another great curve of the river where on the far bank the long low profile of Linton Church will be seen. This handsome church, sometimes called the Cathedral of the Dales, never had a tower, only a small belfry. It dates from the 12th century, and can be reached, when the river is low, by an ancient parishioners' way across worn stepping stones.

Otherwise the Dales Way turns right through a kissing gate which leads into Mill Lane, past Grassington's old Manorial Corn Mill (now private houses) and a trout farm fed by the powerful spring clearly visible in the fish ponds draining from under Grassington Moor. This spring once powered a small lead smelting mill.

A stile on the left some 100 metres above the mill (ignore the gate) gives access once more to the riverside path which descends, through more stiles, to Linton Falls, a series of spectacular rapids and waterfalls over water carved limestone, another manifestation of the Craven Fault. The modern houses on the opposite bank were built on the site of a textile mill, originally water powered, a site under continuous use as a mill since Norman times until it closed in the 1950s.

The mill's extended weir and part of the race, later used for hydro-electric power, can be seen above the Falls. The footbridge over the river at this point, built to link the mill with the village of Grassington (known as "Tin Bridge" because it was once a wooden bridge plated with iron) provides a fine viewing platform for the falls. Dippers are usually to be seen in and out of the water. A narrow, paved path to the right, known by generations of Grassington children as the Snake Walk because of its meandering nature, leads uphill through kissing gates to the main Grassington car park and National Park Centre. Turn left to the centre of Grassington and the village square.

If you are catching the bus 71/72 back to Skipton it stops from the little lay-by opposite the Post Office sorting office (former bus station). Walkers waiting by the timetables in the former bus station at the opposite side of the road have been known to watch it sail by.

If on the other hand you are heading for Linton Youth Hostel, continue over the "Tin" bridge turning right past the former mill house and keep ahead to the lane and the road junction, turning left uphill. Linton village is less than a mile away.

UPPER WHARFEDALE
GRASSINGTON to BUCKDEN

11.5 miles (18 km)

Break points

Kettlewell 7 miles (11 km) – bus 71, 800
Starbotton 9.5 miles (15 km) – bus 71, 800

Grassington, with its ancient cottages and shops crowded around a cobbled Market Square, is one of the most popular tourist villages in the Yorkshire Dales, and justifiably so.

But its past reflects a world very different from the idyllic image recorded by the photographer and painter of the late 20th century. The village we see today essentially reflects a 17th and 18th century industrial community which arose as a result of the intensive, commercial exploitation of the rich veins of lead ore which for centuries were worked and smelted on Grassington Moor high above the village.

However, Grassington has even older origins. The remarkably extensive remains of an Iron Age settlement can still be traced on nearby Lea Green, close to where the Dales Way passes, whilst the village has probably occupied its present site on a well drained limestone terrace above the River Wharfe since Anglian times. The old pump in the square was once the village water supply, taking water from a moorland stream which still runs underneath the village in a culvert.

Though the medieval market has long been discontinued, Grassington had an annual fair or feast which continued as a remnant funfair in the square until recent times, now only surviving as a local children's sports day still held by villagers in October.

Ironically, it was probably the economic hardship resulting from the decline and eventual closure of the Grassington Moor lead mines towards the end of last century that has retained the picturesque village visitors and local residents so value today. There wasn't any cash around to pull down or to improve the cramped miners' cottages, in many cases dating back to the 17th and 18th centuries, which were built around narrow courts or folds. Today these are highly prized bijou residences which now give Grassington so much of its charm.

The coming of the Yorkshire Dales Railway – the Grassington Branch – from Skipton in the early 20th century brought tourists in ever larger numbers to admire the former mining village which now had the patina of age and charm. Excursion trains brought huge numbers of visitors from Leeds, Bradford, Manchester, East Lancashire to the old Grassington Station in Threshfield as late as the mid 1960s. The station site is now a housing estate, whilst the station hotel – the old Wilson's Arms, is now an old people's home. However, the railway still survives as a mineral line as far as Swinden Quarry.

Numbers of tourists increased greatly in the second half of the 20th century as transport and especially roads, improved, with the coming of the bus, the coach and above all the car. Grassington is now a focal point for largely car-based visitor activity. Shops, cafes, pubs, and a choice of accommodation make it a venue for day and weekend visitors alike and a popular base for car touring.

But Grassington is also an excellent starting point for a wide range of moorland and riverside walks. There is a National Park Centre in the main car park on Hebden Road and the excellent Upper Wharfedale Museum in the square in two former lead miners' cottages gives graphic insight into life as it was lived in the village last century and in the first decades of the present.

The village is also reasonably well served by bus, with a regular local bus service to and from Skipton (Keighley & District 71/72; some buses linking with trains at Skipton station) though services are sparse on Sunday mornings and on Sundays in winter. However, the direct Dalesbus 800 from Leeds, Bradford and Ilkley provides an excellent spring and summer weekend service to Grassington and the Upper Dale.

The Dales Way leaves Grassington along its Main Street, turning left in front of the Town Hall along Chapel Street. Almost at the bottom of this street is Town Head Farm, a lovely Jacobean farmhouse with mullioned windows (SE 002644). The Dales Way goes through the farmyard past barns, and then alongside the wall to the right, climbing steadily through a gateway and keeping ahead to a stile. Keep slightly left to the next stile, ahead to the next stile and into a long pasture known as Lea Green. In this and adjacent fields traces of the Iron Age settlement and field pattern can still be seen, though it is best observed either after light snow, during the late afternoon or from the air. The path crosses the pasture keeping directly ahead, with the long field wall about 200 metres to the right, across Lea Green.

The wood visible from here on the left is Grass Wood, a mainly deciduous wood on limestone. This is an exceptionally fine nature reserve, nationally known for its orchids, as well as for primroses, violets, lilies of the valleys, rare shrubs. Not suprisingly it is now an important regional nature reserve and its wildlife and flowers are strictly protected.

You'll see some superb exposed limestone beds in the crags ahead and to the left above Dib Scar. This is an area where, in spring, a delightful variety of wild flowers are to be seen including

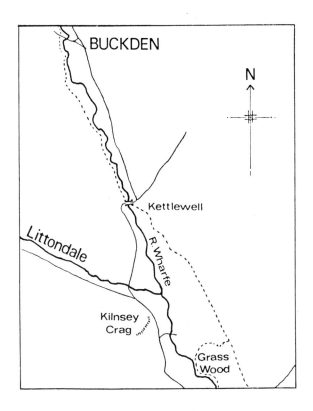

yellow mountain pansies, cowslips and the lovely pink and yellow
bird's eye primrose, an alpine plant remarkably common on the
limestone pastures of the Yorkshire Dales. This is also a good
place to see hares racing in spring whilst plover and curlew circle
overhead over the open pastures.

Where the long wall on the right finally bears diagonally left,
look for a stile in the wall (SD 996664). Cross, near an old dew
pond, crossing the corner of a pasture to the next stile, the path
then ascends gently past a large field lime kiln. These were once
common features in the Dales, in use till the end of last century
before large scale quarrying made lime cheaper, when limestone
was burned in situ with wood, charcoal or coal to make quicklime
and slaked lime for fertiliser.

The Dales Way keeps the same direction, crossing a series of
broad open fields, the line of route marked by ladder stiles, soon
approaching more scars, this time the top of Conistone Dib, a
deep limestone ravine. The Dales Way traverses the top of the
Dib through gates, (SD 993683) soon crossing track which runs

along the line of an ancient monastic way, an old bridleway known as Scot Gate or Bycliffe Road which leads from Kilnsey, where Fountains Abbey had a grange, over Conistone Moor into Nidderdale.

But the Dales Way continues past the tall cross roads signpost, along a narrow, limestone shelf above the valley past the television mast, past a series of outcrops known as Hill Castle Scar, one of which, Conistone Pie, a tower-like structure, looks like it is man-made, but is in fact a natural feature apart from the cairn on its summit.

This is one of the most spectacular sections of the Dales Way – superb, high level walking past ancient enclosures and old ridge ploughing terraces or lynchets, medieval in origin. There are panoramic views into and across the valley below, past the confluence of the River Wharfe and into its tributary valley, Littondale, fed by the little River Skirfare. A notable landmark to the south is Kilnsey Crag, a vast limestone crag undercut by the action of glaciation, its overhang now a challenge to climbers.

The Dales Way keeps its height, now passing the wooded Swinber Scar, even climbing slightly through high enclosures, the path now clearly visible on the ground and marked by stiles. It eventually reaches an area of woodland and joins a track known as Highgate Leys Lane (SD 982706). Turn left down here, through a gate and stile, descending to join the narrow back lane to Kettlewell just before the wooded estate at Scargill. Turn right along this lane.

Scargill House is an Anglican study retreat, and the tall, Scandinavian style roof of its chapel makes a notable landmark.

Follow the lane for about 400 metres past a bench to where the path bends slightly. A sign and a fieldgate indicate the path on the right (SD 975714). Turn left almost immediately through the next gate on the left, the path going along the far side of a wall through a series of stiles. After the second (look for the waymark) the path crosses back to the left hand side of the wall, through more stiles. Keep ahead, the wall now on your left. As you approach Kettlewell village a ladder stile leads into the green track on the left behind cottages. Follow it to Kettlewell church and bear right into the village centre.

Kettlewell, a compact cluster of grey stone houses and cottages in a dramatic setting of green fells, probably takes its name from an early Norse settler, Ketel. Like Grassington this, too, is a former lead mining settlement, and a number of mining cottages remain along the sides of Cam Beck, a narrow tributary valley which flows from the slopes of Great Whernside; most of them are now weekend or holiday cottages.

It is another extremely popular tourist and walkers' centre, crowded at weekends. There's a choice of inns, shops and cafes, and important for Dales Way walkers, bed and breakfast establishments and a youth hostel. Well known walks from here include the ascent of Great Whernside, at 704 metres the highest peak in Wharfedale, or over Old Cote Moor to Arncliffe in Littondale. There are also a number of caves and potholes in the area, the best known being Dowber Gill.

If Kettlewell rather than Buckden is chosen to end this stage, it means another 4.5 miles (7 km) to add to the next day's walk the following day.

From Kettlewell the Dales Way is once again a riverside path, the route starting from the far side of the New Bridge, the bridge carrying the busy B6160 over the Wharfe (SD 9677723). The path crosses a stile on the right to follow a narrow ledge along the riverbank, soon bearing slightly left into an enclosed track, past a barn, and past a series of low lying fields. The path is fairly easy to find, the only less-than-obvious point is where it zigzags right past a gate (SD 958733) to follow the wall to a stile. It now follows the river past its serpentine bends, over more stiles, and alongside the river.

This is a valley whose sides become ever steeper, a classic U-shaped glaciated valley with a flat bottom which is often, during winter, after heavy rain or melting snows, flooded to form a series of shallow lakes, recalling what it must have looked like in late glacial times.

The next village is Starbotton, reached from the Dales Way across a footbridge. This bridge was recently restored with help from the West Riding Ramblers' Association in memory of Harry Smith of Leeds, a lifelong rambler, campaigner for the countryside and lover of the Yorkshire Dales who for many years was secretary of the West Riding Ramblers' Association.

Starbotton is another compact Dales village, its curious name derived from the poles or standards which were cut from coppiced woods nearby. In the 17th century, the village was almost completely destroyed in a devastating flash flood when, after heavy rain, Cam Gill Beck overflowed. An ancient track known as the Walden Road ascends the shoulder of Buckden Pike for Walden, a beautiful cul-de-sac tributary valley of Wensleydale.

The Dales Way heads north-westwards, again an easy to follow route at first along the riverside, but soon leaving the river and following another narrow enclosed path between drystone walls, crossing a footbridge and passing a fine old barn before bearing left to joining an estate track through handsome ornamental woodlands.

This estate, and indeed much of the land passed by the Dales in Upper Wharfedale and Langstrothdale, is now owned and managed by the National Trust, thanks to the generous gift by Graham Watson in memory of his late brother. Graham Watson's work for National Parks and the countryside over a long and active life would be monument enough – but the gift of an estate in the heartland of the Yorkshire Dales, through the National Trust to the nation in perpetuity, reflects a vision and generosity of spirit of rare quality.

Follow the track for some 400 metres. Just after the point where the river comes close to this track, (SD 939765) the Dales Way bears right (signed) over stiles to join and follow the elevated river floodbank to Buckden Bridge. 250 metres along the lane to the right is Buckden village.

Buckden is the site of a former hunting lodge and probably small settlement of keepers in the medieval forest or reserve of Langstrothdale Chase, its name literally derived from the hunt – the wood of the buck or deer.

As the last village of Wharfedale at the bottom of steep passes into Wensleydale, it still has the feeling of an outstation, with an attractive village green, a pub, the Buck Inn, and the last shop and post office until Dentdale. This is yet another farming and former lead mining community serving mines deep into Buckden Pike, the hillside which climbs steeply above the village. Tourism has now replaced lead mining as the way of supplementing incomes, with a choice of bed and breakfast provision and self catering cottages.

It is also the terminus of the Upper Wharfedale bus with the schoolday teatime bus (71) of real value for Dales Way walkers returning to Grassington or Skipton, as well as the Dalesbus 800.

ACROSS THE WATERSHED
BUCKDEN to LEA YEAT

17.5 miles (29 km)

Break points

Cam Houses 9.5 miles (14 km)
Gearstones/Ribblehead 14 miles (20 km)
— Rail from Ribblehead

This is a long and in many respects fairly arduous section of the Dales Way with few facilities along the route. It can be tough going in bad weather if, as so often happens, there is a head wind. So make sure you've good protective clothing and adequate spare food with you before leaving Buckden. In fine weather, however, the views are glorious and there is a real feeling of the Dales Way crossing through mountainous country over the roof and watershed of England.

For day walkers Ribblehead Station, one mile (2km) from the Dales Way at Gearstones, makes an excellent finish and start point, with an extra four miles on the fairly easy day into Sedbergh.

From Buckden Bridge the Dales Way continues along the riverside via a fieldgate on the right, again crossing to the riverside. This is pleasant, gentle walking following the river as it loops round, over stiles, to re-emerge in the lane below Hubberholme by a barn. Turn right along the lane to Hubberholme.

Hubberholme is the point where Upper Wharfedale changes its name to Langstrothdale, a name meaning "long valley" with strong Viking associations, as are other hamlet names along this valley, indicating the settlement pattern of the Vikings who came to northern England via Ireland and Dublin in the tenth century and settled many of the heads of valleys in the western Dales.

The first of these communities is Hubberholme itself with its sturdy church dedicated to the Anglo-Saxon Christian King of Northumbria, Saint Oswald. Dating from the 13th century and like many medieval churches in the Dales, it was built to give a degree of protection against marauding Scots.

It is also one of the few churches in England to have a rood loft, an early Tudor, pre-Reformation screen above the altar, carved with a badge of the Percies, Lords of Northumberland. It is said that this loft survived in remote Langstrothdale because Cromwell's men never travelled as far as this point. The ashes of the great Yorkshire noveliest, playwright and broadcaster J.B. Priestley lie scattered in the vicinity, Hubberholme being one of Priestley's favourite corners of England.

The little inn opposite the church, The George, was like many inns once owned by the church and a curious ritual is still carried out here every New Year when the rent of a piece of pasture behind the inn is auctioned off to the highest bidder, the income used to help the poor of the parish. Whoever puts in the highest bid by the time the candle is burnt out to a stub gets the use of the land.

The Dales Way continues through the fieldgate at the side of the church, along the path which continues behind the church (SD 926783) and along a hillside where a landslip some years ago blocked the path which remains narrow. It soon descends to the riverside once again. The River Wharfe is now little more than a turbulent stream, tumbling through a shallow, rocky gorge. The path follows the riverside, through stiles, across pasture, eventually reaching the sheep folds of a farm where little gates lead behind the farm and into the hamlet of Yockenthwaite with its handsome stone bridge and lovely Georgian farmhouse.

The Dales Way continues up the valley, over a crossing track and bearing slightly right, behind the field wall to a gate, the path soon descending again to the riverside, by narrow fields through a gateway and over another stile. In the next field (SD 899794) you pass the remains of a Bronze Age stone circle. This is Yockenthwaite Stone Circle, consisting of some 30 stones, some fallen, some standing, their purpose and origin unknown, but quite possibly a little place of worship on an already busy cross-Pennine trade route. This part of the Dales Way has been in use for rather a long time.

The path keeps along the river then bears slightly right across meadows, (follow the waymarks) over stiles to a bridge into Deepdale Farm. Keep ahead below the farm and along the farm drive, down to the lane by Deepdale Bridge. Cross the bridge, and continue upstream along the track along the southern bank of the river.

The Wharfe is now a series of shallow waterfalls between shallow grassy banks, a popular picnic place on summer afternoons. Keep ahead past New House, a farm cottage, soon passing more falls as the river veers to the west below the road, finally emerging at Beckermonds by the footbridge.

The name Beckermonds is pure Anglo-Saxon in origin, remarkably similar to modern German, meaning the mouth of the becks or streams – corrupted in at least one gravestone in Hubberholme Churchyard to Beggarman's. Turn right along the lane back to the Langstrothdale road.

From here, as a hostile notice on a gate will remind you, the Dales Way has no off-road route, and it's just over three quarters of a mile (1.2 kilometres) of tarmac. This road can be busy in summer and on Sunday afternoons so keep to the right and take care – luckily the nature of the road means that most traffic if unpleasant is at least slow-moving. Without traffic, it is in fact a pretty route, climbing above a narrow gorge past a little roadside spring before descending again past Oughtershaw Hall and into Oughtershaw itself. The little former school building on the right, now a hostel, was originally designed, in Venetian style, by the great Victorian art historian and essayist John Ruskin.

Until recently the telephone kiosk in Oughtershaw was the only telephone in the hamlet, so that it has a loud bell outside. If anyone received an incoming call the bell rings and whoever answers has to bring the recipient of the call in from farm or field to the phone booth. The Celtic-style cross in the hamlet's centre was erected to commemorate Queen Victoria's Golden Jubilee in 1887.

The Dales Way now bears off to the left at the junction of tracks past the hamlet (SD 868816) along a lonely farm track. Ahead is Nethergill and beyond Swarthgill Farm, both remote sheep farms, the latter with its scattering of trees looking like the end of the world. Keep ahead to and beyond both farms past which the Dales Way continues to climb slowly upwards, now crossing over rough pasture by the often welcome shelter of a field wall, towards Far End Barn and Breadpiece Barn (SD 830822) ahead.

The tiny stream you have been following to the left, now known as Oughtershaw Beck, is in fact the source of the River Wharfe, and on the hillside opposite, on the summit of Oughtershaw Moss, is the spring out of the moorland from which this great river emerges, little more than a narrow boggy ravine or syke.

Only a few tens of metres to the west over the boggy saddle of the fells lie seeps which form the sources of Cam Beck, a tributary of the River Ribble which flows into the Irish Sea rather than the North Sea into which the Wharfe eventually reaches. This is the watershed of all England.

Breadpiece Barn owes its name to its curious shape, like a loaf. A welcoming sign by the stile – if it survives – promises refreshment ahead. The route bears right, up the slope, towards Cam Houses, ever finer views as you ascend.

You finally reach one of the highest farms in the Dales at Cam Houses, where Dales Way walkers can usually find welcoming refreshment either at the farmhouse or in the barn, and, by prior arrangement, bed and breakfast and a Bunkhouse Barn.

From Cam Houses the route goes between and past the farm buildings, but leaves the main track which climbs to the right to keep ahead over a stile and to the forestry plantation ahead. From here the route has been unofficially diverted (formal diversion pending – don't try to enter the forest) to follow the forest fence uphill, turning left over a stile above the forest, then bearing right

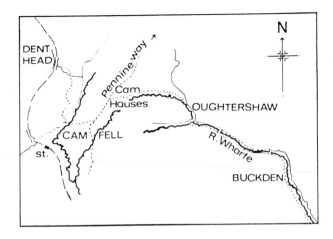

up the open pasture to a stile (SD 816818) beyond which leads onto the Cam Fell High Road joined at the Dales Way cairn.

The Cam High Road is part of the old Roman Road between Ribchester and Bainbridge built by Julius Agricola in the First Century to tame the warlike Brigantes. It also carries the 250 mile Pennine Way, Britain's oldest National Trail, which runs between Edale in the Derbyshire Peak District and Scotland. Sadly, it also carries an increasing number of four wheel drive vehicles which have now seriously damaged the metalled surface of this Roman highway.

In good weather the views from the Cam High Road are breathtaking, and include not only a splendid panorama of the Three Peaks – Penyghent, Ingleborough and Whernside – but also the great multi-arched Ribblehead viaduct on the Settle-Carlisle railway, a magnificent enginering feat on a scale to match the epic grandeur of the landscape. In bad weather this is also one of the most exposed places in all England, with storms coming straight off the Irish Sea into the faces of Dales Way walkers. At least it is downhill from this point – fast easy walking along the metalled track – if you need to hurry to shelter and the comforts of civilisation.

The Dales Way follows the Cam High Road down to Cam End (SD 802804), a cairn where the Pennine Way bears off to the left into Ribblesdale. But the Dales Way continues steeply down the metalled highway to Gayle Beck. Here a recently improved ford and long footbridge crosses Gayle Beck, the main tributary source of the Ribble. A track leads from the ford up to the gate into the main Hawes-Ingleton road, the B6255. Turn left along the road for Gearstones.

The scattered communities between Ribblehead and Gearstones

can hardly be said to even constitute a hamlet. In both the 18th and the 19th centuries, however, the situation was very different. At Gearstones there was an inn, part of which still survives, now a roadside farmhouse offering bed and breakfast and some bunkhouse and camping facilities.

This was one of the most important Drovers' inns in the north of England, where Scottish drovers would spend the night whilst bringing down huge herds of cattle on foot along the Drove roads from the Scottish Uplands (mainly Galloway and Ayrshire) to the cattle markets of the English Midlands. Many were too poor to afford a room in the inn, but would sleep rough wrapped in their great tartan plaids, entertaining themselves in the evenings around camp fires with eating, drinking and dancing.

The trade ceased abruptly when the Settle-Carlisle railway was opened in the 1870s, though the inn lingered on until the 1939-45 war.

It's about a mile and a half from here (2 km) to Ribblehead where there is a railway station and pub offering bed and breakfast and meals. Trains operate from here to Settle, Skipton and Leeds and from the new northbound platform, to Appleby and Carlisle – services are available daily, though not on Sundays from the beginning of November until the end of March. At weekends the area is busy with parked cars and lines of walkers undertaking the over-popular Three Peaks Walk.

Activity of a very different kind was to be seen on Batty Moss around what is now Ribblehead viaduct, about a mile down the valley, when, in the 1870s the mighty Midland Railway was pushing its main line northwards to Scotland. Here developed a series of shanty villages housing a vast army of navvies to build the great 24 arch 165 foot high viaduct and the adjacent 2,629 yards long Blea Moor Tunnel. Many of the workers were Irish but others came also from Devon, Scotland and from the Dales lead mining communities which were already declining. Traces of the villages, which had Wild West, biblical or military names such as Jericho, Sebastopol, can still be seen on the moor together with the tram-ways used in building the viaduct. Over 1,000 lives were lost through accidents, and disease in one of the last major railway schemes in Britain to be built almost entirely by manual labour.

The Dales Way turns right before Gearstones, just beyond the point where the old turnpike becomes unenclosed, (SD 783802), following the farmtrack to Winshaw Farm (B&B) but then continuing uphill outside the farm wall, and to the right, along the edge of the moor, outside the enclosure wall.

The path, clearly marked, offers fine views across a bleak, and largely treeless upland of open moors. Keep ahead, past Gate Cote and above High Gayle Farm, where the path bears left along an old track, crossing the beck and patch of bog at a footbridge, then clinging to the side of the moor (the old track along the bottom is wet in places). Cross stiles, then ahead over Stoops Moss to a stile in the Dentdale Road from Newby Head.

At the time of writing, the Dales Way follows the lane downhill, under the majestic Denthead Viaduct.

This impressive viaduct is built of "black" limestone (which is ordinary Carboniferous limestone with a high carbon content) and is 100 feet high and has ten arches along its 197 feet length. This lane above the viaduct is a favourite vantage point for photographers taking shots of the occasional steam special as well as the modern blue and grey Super Sprinter trains.

The Dales Way follows the lane alongside the little River Dee into Dentdale, soon passing Denthead Youth Hostel, in a fine Victorian house. Walking on tarmac (the road is usually quiet) is here amply compensated by the intimate beauty of the valley, with river, trees and quiet farms sharing the narrow gorge, the railway along the fellside high above. The junction with the track from Artengill, another fine piece of railway architecture crossing a narrow gill, which carries the old track from Widdale and Hawes. Also built of black marble, Artengill viaduct has eleven arches and is 117 feet high.

Just below the Artengill Viaduct is the site of a long vanished water-powered marble works, Dentdale black marble being highly prized last century for use as an ornamental stone for table tops and fireplaces, its many fossils gleaming a pale grey when polished. A young Tyneside engineer known as William Armstrong came on a walking holiday to Dentdale with his wife in the 1830s, and fascinated with the waterwheel conceived the idea of creating a more efficient form of harnessing that power – the turbine. Armstrong went on to found the great Newcastle engineering and shipbuilding dynasty that bore his name, the turbine principle perhaps being one of the most significant engineering discoveries of all time.

The Dales Way continues past the 18th century Sportsman's Inn – which welcomes walkers and offers bed and breakfast. At Lea Yeat, where in former times there was a Quaker meeting house, a lane to the right zigzags up a 1 in 4 hill to Dent Station, England's highest main line railway station at 1,150 feet above sea level, and a useful starting or finishing point for anyone walking the Dales Way in day stages – but allow at least 20 minutes for the ascent from Lea Yeat.

An alternative route into Dentdale which is being examined as a possible route for the Dales Way to reduce road walking, though with more climbing, turns right at the Newby Head road for 400 metres to where a gate leads to a bridleway marked, intriguingly "BW Dead End" (SD 791835). This is in fact Galloway Gate, part of an ancient droving road which led from Scotland to the Yorkshire Dales and was used by Scottish Drovers heading for Gearstones in large numbers. Where the official bridleway ends

(SD793848), a stile and a gate leads to a lovely sunken green way, soon with open views along Widdale, before the way veers left down and follows the wall down over Swineley Coum to join the Widdale Road, an unsurfaced track, at a gate (SD 793862). Though this section is not currently on the Definitive Map, its status was agreed to be public as part of the proposed Pennine Bridleway – for further news see the Dales Way handbook. Turn left down the steep, stony track which descends Arten Gill, soon going under Arten Gill viaduct and rejoining the present Dales Way south of the Sportsman's Inn. If you are heading for Dent Station however, maintain your height by continuing up and along Gallowgate, the green way directly ahead from the junction with Widdale Road, which climbs over Cross Wold below Great Knoutberry, with superb views over Whernside, Great Coum and the Howgills. Turn left at the junction with the tarmaced Coal Road and descend to Dent Station.

DENTDALE
LEA YEAT TO SEDBERGH

11 miles (17 km)

Break point

Dent 4.5 miles (7 km)

Dentdale is one of the most intimately beautiful of the Yorkshire Dales, or, as some people would have it, Cumbrian Dales, as since 1974 it has been part of Cumbria, though most Dent people consider themselves to be a native of the White Rose – the old West Riding of Yorkshire.

Perhaps because it is westward facing, it has a gentle, more sheltered aspect, hedgerows rather than drystone walls which in spring are filled with primroses, violets, campion, blackthorn.

From Lea Yeat bridge (SD 761878), the Dales Way takes the stile to the left and follows the River Dee, along a rocky, narrow riverside path. Much of the river here and further along the valley runs dry in the summer or after a period without rain, the stream following subterranean passageways and cave systems through the water-carved limestone, only to re-emerge with irrepressible energy after heavy rainfall.

The chapel with a small bell tower on the right, across the river by the trees, is Cowgill Chapel, its name reflecting a curious dispute in the 1860s when Professor Adam Sedgwick (1785-1873), the great Victorian geologist who was born in Dent, wrote a booklet known as *The Memorial by the Trustees of Cowgill Chapel* which claimed that through an administrative error the chapel had been wrongly named Kirkthwaite. Queen Victoria, a close personal friend of Professor Sedgwick from the time when Sedgwick had worked with Prince Albert on University reforms, intervened in the dispute and an Act of Parliament was passed in 1869 to restore the ancient name of Cowgill.

Sedgwick wrote a subsequent pamphlet *Supplement to the Memorial* (etc) which, like its predecessor, was filled with notes on local geology and history and personal anecdote. Together the two pamphlets constitute a remarkable record of a Yorkshire dale as it was in Sedgwick's boyhood at the end of the 18th century at a time when new factories in the West Riding were destroying the cottage hand-knitting industry and the "terrible" (ie fast and furious) knitters of Dent were soon to be no more.

The Dales Way rejoins the lane at Ewegales Bridge and follows

The Dales Way runs diagonally across this picture as it follows the valley floor between Kettlewell and Buckden.

Daffodils add early spring colour to the centre of Buckden.

Sheep-shearing is a feature of Buckden Gala, held annually in June.

Langstrothdale as viewed from the crags above Buckden. The River Wharfe lazily snakes its way down-dale from Hubberholme.

The old bridge at Yockenthwaite, close to one of the most attractive stretches of the River Wharfe.

Beckermonds at the head of Langstrothdale.

*Empty expanses of moorland surround Ribblehead, venue
for a sheep show each September.*

The Sportsman's Arms, a useful stopping point for thirsty walkers in upper Dentdale.

The classic view of Sedbergh and the Howgills.

Sedbergh is surrounded by ancient bridges. This example is to the south of the town.

The Dales Way runs alongside the River Lune at the point where it is crossed by the Sedbergh to Kendal road.

Journey's end! The glistening waters of the Windermere can seem like a foretaste of paradise to the weary rambler.

Bowness boasts both a promanade and landing stages.

the lane for 300 metres before once again taking a lovely, meandering footpath which begins at a gate almost facing you as the lane bends right. (SD 752867). This crosses pasture below Rivling Farm, entering a conifer plantation over stiles. It continues through dense woods to Little Town, going over ladder stiles, outside and below the farm before re-entering the woods, bearing left to leave the wood over stiles and along a wallside. The path then crosses a pasture – look for waymarks and signs asking you to walk in single file, below Birchen Tree and Hackerfall, before entering the farm track and turning right at Coat Faw. The Way then cuts across the corner of a pasture at Coat Faw over ladder stiles, above the wall around the outside of Clint, but below West Clint, and along the wall and the top of the field through more stiles to a barn at Laithbank. Turn right here down to the lane.

A feature of Dentdale is that because it is an old Viking settlement there are few villages and hamlets, but isolated "statesman's" or yeoman farmsteads, the dale being originally divided in a Norse, democratic fashion with long, narrow farms, each containing its share of good bottom meadow land and higher poor pasture.

Turn left along the lane for 200 metres to where at the second gate right (signed) the Dales Way crosses the pasture to a tiny plank bridge in a gully known as Lenny's Leap beyond which the path reaches the riverside at Nelly Bridge, a footbridge across a rocky gorge of the Dee where there are fantastic limestone formations to be seen. The Way then follows the riverside over a series of high stiles to Tommy Bridge (who Lenny, Nelly and Tommy were is lost in history) by a ford (SD 725864). From here the way turns left through a gate but don't take the next gate ahead, but bear left to a narrow gap stile in the wall on the left. The path now follows a wall up the hillside, then, keeping the same direction crosses a low hillock to descend into the wall corner and a stile into the lane by Mill Bridge.

At the farm here, in the early 19th century, there was a "Knitting School" where local children learned the techniques of hand knitting. Both men and women knitted the rough but hard-wearing local wool from Swaledale or Herdwick sheep when tending flocks or undertaking housework, or on winter evenings around the peat or fell coal fire to supplement otherwise meagre incomes. Most of the vast quantity of woollen gloves, hats and stockings produced by the "Terrible Knitters" were sold at Kendal market, sometimes supplying the military with winter gloves.

The Dales Way follows the path down Deepdale Beck, a tributary of the Dee, along floodbanks, over stiles, to its confluence with the River Dee, then alongside the Dee itself, over a little footbridge and along the floodbanks before bearing left to the bridge over Keld Beck, then right by the stream to Church Bridge below Dent. Turn left along the lane into the village.

Dent Town, to give its correct name, is one of the loveliest and

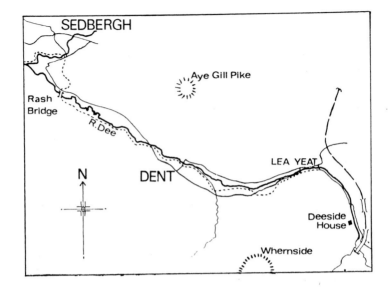

least spoiled of all Dales villages with its narrow, winding cobbled main street, and narrow colour washed cottages which once had balconies where local people would knit and chat to each other across the narrow street.

You'll see the great fountain of pinkish grey Shap granite in the village centre. It was placed there by local people as a permanent, fitting memorial to Adam Sedgwick, a great benefactor to his native Dale simply inscribed with his name; his dates were added later, because everyone who mattered in the Dale knew who he was and didn't need a reminder. There is also a memorial to Sedgwick and other members of his family (Sedgwick is still a common Dentdale family name) in the church, though he was actually buried in Norwich, and the little grammar school where Sedgwick was taught by his father, the vicar, before going on to complete his studies at Sedbergh School and Trinity College, Cambridge University, survives behind the church.

The Church itself dates from Norman times with a Norman doorway (now blocked) but is mostly late Perpendicular, (early 16th century), with a square 18th century tower, heavily restored in the 19th century. The pulpit is partially 17th century and there are some 17th century pews. Gravestones in the churchyard include memorials to the Sill family of what is now Whernside Manor whose dealings with the slave trade and related scandals is thought by some scholars to be the inspiration for part of Emily Brontë's *Wuthering Heights*.

Dent has two inns, the George and Dragon and the Sun, both

of which sell locally brewed Dent Bitter. There are cafes, restaurants, shops – including a post office – and a choice of bed and breakfast establishments and a camp site.

Local transport is somewhat sporadic from Dent, with local schoolbuses down to Sedbergh (but no onward further connections); there are occasional National Park sponsored buses in the summer months. However, local taxi operators offer a cut price fare up to Dent Station – enquire locally.

The Dales Way leaves Dent by the riverside, reached by turning down a narrow path to the right, some 50 metres beyond the car park (SD 704871), then left along the riverside.

This path again follows the flood embankment rejoining the road for a few metres before again following the riverside to Barth Bridge. The Way continues along the same side of the river by a stile at the bridge across stiles and a footbridge; the River Dee here a lazy, more sluggish kind of river, lined with willows, a haven for a variety of ducks and waders.

If you look up to the hillside to the left you'll notice a distinct change in the landscape occuring. The Dent Fault crosses the valley about this point, the typical Carboniferous limestones and sandstones of the Yorkshire Dales yielding to the older, harder Silurian slates and shales of the Lake District, a difference which is soon apparent in building style and drystone walls. The colour and form and even vegetation of the landscape change noticeably as you pass the line of fault, first described by Adam Sedgwick in the 1830s. A certain instability on the hillside, including landslips, is caused by the fault line, roughly marked by the road from Barbon and by Helms Knot, the round green hill to the north.

The riverside path eventually emerges in the narrow lane at Ellers, and the Dales Way follows this virtually traffic-free farm road up past Rottenbutts Wood and Brackensgill to Rash Bridge. A few metres up the lane is Rash Mill, an 18th century watermill which still has its waterwheel in place, recently restored by boys from Sedbergh School.

The Dales Way crosses the river by turning right over at Rash Bridge (SD 660899) turning right again into the Sedbergh road for 100 metres where just past a milestone a gate on the left leads into a long field. Climb directly up the field bearing left to a stile at the top. Continue to where a second stile leads into a green lane (SD 662904). Turn left along a track which crosses the edge of Long Rigg where, above the old golf course, there is a spectacular panoramic view of the town of Sedbergh, set against a backcloth of the green-domed Howgill Fells.

The track winds down the hillside and through the hamlet of Millthrop. Keep ahead across Millthrop's old stone bridge over the River Rawthey, following the road left and uphill into Sedbergh town.

Sedbergh enjoys a magnificent position immediately below the southern ramparts of the Howgills, with one particular hill, Winder, dominating the town. Though most of the town is relatively modern, some old parts of the town remain, most notably some old Tudor shops and courtyards off the Main Street, where, down quiet alleyways, weavers' galleries are still to be seen.

That the town once had strategic importance is revealed by the fact that a grassy mound immediately behind the town is the site of a Norman motte-and-bailey castle which guarded what was an important pass across the Pennines, now followed by the A684 between Kendal and Richmond. The little National Park Centre in Sedbergh (open daily in summer) occupies a former wool shop which according to a reputable source was where playwright George Bernard Shaw bought his socks, being the only shop he knew in England that would supply socks for his left and his right feet.

It was to Sedbergh that a certain George Fox, son of a Leicestershire weaver, made his way in 1652 after his great vision on Pendle Hill, Lancashire, preaching on the day of Sedbergh Hiring Fair outside the Parish Church. Soon afterwards, having stayed overnight with his friend Richard Robinson, Fox preached a inspirational sermon to over a thousand "seekers" on nearby Firkbank Fell, standing on a rock still marked as Fox's Pulpit. These seekers were told to spread the word far and wide, and it was from this moment that the Quaker Movement or Society of Friends, as it came to be known, was established. Despite much suffering and persecution the Quaker faith became strongly established in both Britain and the United States and has an enormous, still continuing influence.

St. Andrews Parish Church, Sedbergh, is a particularly fine Dales church, with work from many different medieval periods – Norman and 13th and 14th century work predominating. There is a memorial to John Dawson, the Garsdale shepherd mathematician who was one the finest teachers of mathematics of his day, tutor to Adam Sedgwick.

Sedbergh is also celebrated for its Sedbergh School, the village grammar school which during the 18th and 19th centuries expanded to become a major public school whose buildings and playing fields now dominate much of the town.

Like Dent, there is a good choice of inns, shops, cafes and accommodation. But it isn't an easy place to travel to or from; local buses purely serve the needs of residents, with no buses leaving the area after midday – and then only on certain days. A taxi to Garsdale Station is probably the best bet, except those days when National Park or Cumbria County Council sponsored services link with Dent.

Section 5

FROM THE LUNE
TO THE KENT:
SEDBERGH to BURNESIDE

17 miles (28 km)

Break points None

This section is both one of the most rewarding and yet, for some people, most frustrating sections of the Dales Way. It goes through countryside which is relatively little frequented, whose footpaths, apart from the Dales Way, are relatively little used. The path, keeping to the riversides, meanders – you seem to spend a great deal of time getting not very far.

But the rewards are to savour a countryside of a very distinct character and charm. Many Dales Way walkers have suggested that though the scenery is to some people less spectacular than, say, Wharfedale or Dentdale, this remains one of their favourite sections because it is both so quiet and different to what they have experienced before. There are several points, however, where the views, especially of the Howgills and the distant Lakeland fells, are quite breathtaking.

Because this is such a long section, an early start is required – which suggests for most people an overnight stop in Sedbergh. Given the lack of public transport it is a sensible idea even for people planning to do the rest of the walk in day stages to arrange an overnight at this point.

Though there is a limited amount of bed and breakfast in inter-mediate settlements (see the Dales Way handbook), between Sedbergh and Burneside, there are no shops, cafes nor even a pub. So again, it is important not to leave Sedbergh without adequate supplies of food and drink. Whilst the going is fairly easy throughout, pathfinding takes a little more care, though waymarking is much improved in recent years.

You can leave Sedbergh along the main road down to Millthrop Bridge and take the kissing gate on the right just before the bridge, leading through a semi-wooded estate, climbing a wooded knoll and grassy viewpoint, but keeping ahead through stiles across fields below a long hedge to emerge in the lane at Birks (SD 652914). A shorter route from Sedbergh centre with less road walking is to take the enclosed path to the right immediately beyond the church, going between the school playing fields and the church before heading over a stile and between more playing fields to Birks.

Continue past Birks Mill, ignoring the footbridge over the Rawthey, passing the sewage works and continuing along the narrow riverside path which soon becomes an extremely attractive section of wooded riverside. It is the meeting of the two rivers Dee and Rawthey, at a point not far short of where they both join forces with the Lune. The path continues to the Rawthey Viaduct where the old and much lamented Ingleton-Tebay Railway, closed in the 1960s, crosses the Rawthey. The path ascends the embankment (SD 644910) to give splendid views across to Winder and the Howgills before descending back to the riverside and following the river by fields before eventually reaching the main A683 road. Turn left here.

An interesting variation can be made by taking the fieldpath which leaves the riverside before Birks Mill (SD 651914) which crosses over the same embankment to Briggflatts, an unusual early Quaker meeting house, dating from 1675 at a time when the Friends were suffering persecution, and were too poor to fit a ceiling, lining the roof with moss for warmth. The gallery was added in 1711. You can rejoin the main Dales Way by turning left along the main A683 – but walk on the right hand side of the narrow road to face oncoming traffic.

The main Dales Way follows the A683 from the point where the riverside path joins the road for about 600 metres, before a stile on the right (SD 632911) leads to a path by a fence. It crosses a little footbridge over a stream, then bears half left over a little wooded knoll towards a gate and a pleasant green lane which leads to the left to High Oaks Farm, (SD 627911), a 17th century farmhouse which has been largely gentrified. Pass the farmhouse, turning right along a track. Where this track ends, turn right along a hedge and fence to the gate directly gate ahead which leads to a track between tall hedges to Luneside Farm (SD 629918).

Follow the farmtrack past the farm, then through a gate left and along a fence to a stile left and along the riverside pasture close by a new river, the River Lune, over stiles to meet the busy A684 at Lincoln's Inn Bridge, its name indicating a long vanished drover's inn by what was then a ford. Mr Lincoln was the landlord.

Now follow a lovely section of the River Lune, with the green expanse of the Firbank Fells to the left. From Lincoln's Inn Bridge follow the signed path by a gate, ignoring a stile to the left by the riverside which is just a fisherman's path, keep ahead to the gap in the fence and a stile ahead, close by the river. Past the next ladder stile is a shallow ford over Crowsdale Beck where the Dales Way passes the remains of the handsome Lune Viaduct (SD 621930), a beautifully proportioned brick and iron structure, now brooding over the valley like some extravagant, abandoned folly. It was also part of the much lamented Ingleton-Tebay railway. Go under the viaduct before bearing right up the field to cross stiles and into the track leading to Low Branthwaite Farm (SD 634933).

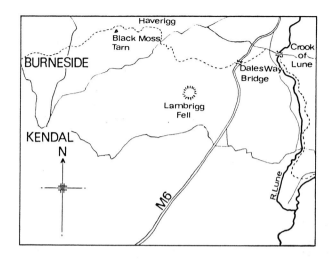

If the ford is impassable after heavy rain, there is an alternative path. Turn right before the ladder stile going along the wall to a stile, then left through the railway underpass to a gate, turning right along the top of a narrow field above to a stile and the track to Low Branthwaite.

The path crosses the farm access road by stiles, following the fence on the left, bearing right with the fence to the top of the field leading into a short length of enclosed track (fine views of the Howgills to the right); where it emerges through gates ignore the track leading Bramaskew Farm (SD 636937) ahead, but turn left through a gap stile, following a fence, crossing to a second stile ahead before descending a large field towards a small barn ahead. Head to the left of this. The path joins a track leading to Nether Bainbridge Farm (SD 632943).

Before reaching the farm, take the stile before a barn on the left (signed). Go right, around the barn, following the path signed to Hole House, and ignoring a small gate, keep ahead to where a gate with a sign indicates the line of the Dales Way over a small hillock from where there are more spectacular views of the Howgills and the Lune valley spread out before you.

You will see Hole House Farm (SD 630945) ahead, nestling in a hollow by the river; descend the long field to it. Go through the farm gate, keeping right by the barns, then bear left past the farmhouse to a small gate. This leads to a footbridge over Smithy Beck. Turn left, taking the lower of two paths which leads over a stile on the left which bears left down to the riverside once again. Follow the riverside over another stile and along a large pasture below Thwaite Farm to cross Chapel Beck at a footbridge, the way now entering a woodland, the route ascending and affording views of a lovely wooded section of riverside. Through a gate, the path enters pasture and continues along the river to where it bears right to a gate just before Crook of Lune bridge (SD 620963).

This narrow stone bridge is barely wide enough for a small car to pass. Offering magnificent views from its parapet both of the Lune Gorge itself and the Howgills, it is oddly reminiscent of Ilkley Bridge at the start of the Dales Way. Until 1974 it marked the exit of the Dales Way from the West Riding of Yorkshire and entry into Westmorland. All is now within Cumbria, though this is still the boundary of the Yorkshire Dales National Park.

Cross the bridge and follow the narrow lane as it ascends past attractive cottages and under the elegant red brick viaduct of the former Ingleton-Tebay railway. Sadly the next couple of miles of the Dales Way is dominated by transport – the intermittent roar of express trains on the electrified West Coast Main line railway between London Euston and Glasgow, and the far more intrusive, and incessant roar and scream of heavy road traffic on the M6.

Turn right in the lane then first left at the crossroads to Beckfoot (SD 615965), before immediately turning left again along a grassy way in front of a cottage, above a stream in a little wooded gill. This climbs to a bend at a stile – cross and go straight ahead here, following a line of trees, keeping ahead before veering to the left away from a cattle path to a stile in the top corner of the long field. Keep ahead through a gate to join the track to Lakethwaite Farm (SD 606958).

Take a stile on the right before the farm buildings, walking outside and around the farm, climbing at first to follow a wall then a fence to a stile in the field corner. The path crosses the next field to a stile in the lane. Turn left for a few metres then over a stile on the right – follow the wall to the bridge that carries a farm track over the M6 motorway.

Don't follow the track ahead to Lambrigg Head but turn immediately left down a path between the motorway and farm buildings which leads to the lane at a stile. Turn left here for 150 metres to a gate on the right (SD598957). Go through, but turn sharp left (avoid the more obvious cattle path directly ahead) to a partially hidden stile in the wall corner.

The path now crosses a field and heads, by stiles and alongside a fence, towards and behind Holme Park, a palatial farmhouse (SD 595956) in a lovely setting. Keep ahead over more stiles which mark the line of path to join a pleasant green way through gates which leads past the walled gardens and in front of Moresdale Hall (SD 5888959). Do not follow the main drive but keep in roughly the same direction along a clear, if somewhat overgrown, path through rhododendrons, gates and into a field. Continue ahead with a fence on your left, crossing a little beck to emerge at a stile in a lane. Turn left along the lane for 400 metres to a cross roads at Thatchmoor Head; turn right here, but go left at a gate opposite a house, following a bridleway along the top of a field which gradually slopes down to a level crossing over the high speed electrified West Coast railway – care is needed to cross the tracks, the watchwords being Stop, Listen and Look.

The Dales Way is now approaching the foothills of the Lake District whose spiky summits form an attractive backdrop to the undulating terrain, and began to dominate the skyline.

The route keeps the same direction from the railway by a low lying pasture and stream (aim to the left of the trees ahead) to join a track which bears left (and can be extremely muddy at times) to Green Head Farm (SD 573966). Now follow the farm drive as it curves left past Green Head, but after about 150 metres, just before the cattle grid and bridge, leave the farm track to follow the streamside path (SD 571964) right, which reaches a pretty foot-bridge and leads to the track past Grayrigg Foot farm to the A685.

Turn right for 100 metres, before taking the farm road on the left leading to Thursgill Farm which descends to Thursgill Beck. Soon past the bridge bear left along the path through a gate, and over a hurdle stile before climbing up to a stile in the field corner. Keep ahead along the edge of the pasture, with a hedge on the left before following a track towards a barn. But take a gate in the facing hedge to follow a path to the left, keeping your height and to the right of a little wooded knoll. Descend into the valley formed by the little River Mint, crossing at a footbridge (SD 562970). Walk ahead to join a lane at a kissing gate. Turn right here. This leads to a Shaw End, a fine colonial style mansion. Look for another kissing gate on the left by a yew tree leading into a parallel track. Beyond a gate is a broad track. Pass a building on the left, then turn left along a green way through a gate and a garden of a private house, High Barn – this is a public right of way. Go over the stile at the end of the garden to follow the track uphill to a lane above Patton Bridge.

Cross here to follow the drive down to Biglands Farm (SD 556973), turning left in front of the house to a stile, then along a narrow pasture; where the field widens out keep left to a stile, and on past a section of collapsed field wall to Black Moss Tarn (SD 548971).

This is a quiet upland pool in a setting of craggy rocks, the haunt of wildgeese and swans; pylons behind the pool sadly spoil the otherwise tranquil atmosphere.

Cross a stile to the right of the tarn, and from its northern bank climb the field behind the pylon, descending to New House Farm below (SD 546973), entering the farm yard and through a gate to the left of the house which leads to a lovely green lane. Follow this due west, heading below Goodham Scales where it joins the farm track. Where the track bears sharp left beyond a gate, go through another gate ahead signed the Dales Way. Keep the same direction down the hillside to join another farm access road at a stile near Garnett's Fold (SD 538968). Follow this track past the farm cottages, soon with Skelsmergh Tarn just visible through trees then past Tarn Bank to descend to the main A6 – a road not as busy as the M6, but with still enough traffic to require considerable care when crossing.

This is the old road from Preston to Scotland, a road with a history, its most notorious moment perhaps after the 1745 rebellion when Bonny Prince Charlie's ill-fated Highlanders were chased up here by Butcher Cumberland's troops after the Battle of Preston, killing any stragglers that were found on the way.

The way now crosses this road and turns left for 50 metres before taking the drive to Burton House Farm (SD 528964). Take the gate ahead and to the left of the house, and a second one immediately to the left of that to cross a small enclosure to another gate before crossing the sloping field to a ladder stile at the far end by an area of marshy ground, then turn sharp right to half hidden stiles and a footbridge over the beck (SD 527963). Continue up the field to a gate from where there's a first view of the town of Kendal, dominated by its grey stone rooftops and on a grassy hilltop, the ruins of the castle, birthplace of Katherine Parr, the one wife of Henry VIII to survive him.

Now bear half left to descend to a stile in the field corner, crossing to another stile just above, following the hedge and wall over three more stiles, the last being on the left, but keep the same direction to locate two more stiles to enter the lane south of Oakbank Cottages (SD 518962). Turn right, but before reaching the cottages go through a gate on the left. Follow the wall until you reach a stile on the left. Cross, keeping to the far side of the wall to reach the banks of the River Sprint at another stile. Keep on the same side of the river past the attractive old mill, bridge and cottages in their woodland setting, and continue to the main Burneside road. Turn right here, continuing for 400 metres to Burneside Hall (SD 510960).

This is a red sandstone peel tower dating back to the 14th century, built to defend the inhabitants against groups of marauding Scots. It forms a fine example of a semi-fortified medieval house with its crenellated tower and gateway, but it is a still working farm and there is no public access.

Turn left at the cross roads past the Hall, noting the pond in the grounds, and passing the Burneside Paper Mill and over the bridge across the River Kent to the centre of Burneside village.

Burneside is really a small industrial community on the outskirts of Kendal dominated by its paper mill. There is a pub and a shop – the first on the Dales Way since Sedbergh. Though there is limited bed and breakfast accommodation in the village, there is an approximately hourly rail service (Burneside Station is 250 metres to the north of the village cross roads) and fairly frequent bus services into Kendal for a wider choice of accommodation, including the Youth Hostel.

Section 6
LAKELAND: BURNESIDE TO BOWNESS
10 miles (16 km)

Break point
Staveley   3.5 miles (6 km) – trains to Burneside, Kendal,
Oxenholme;
buses to Kendal, Lancaster

The last stage of the Dales Way is no anticlimax, but provides a
dramatic and at times quite breathtakingly lovely conclusion to
the whole walk.

Begin at the eastern (Sedbergh) side of Burneside Paper Mill
(SD 506958) by a stile and kissing gate, signed to Bowston, following the path around the perimeter fence of the mill to another
kissing gate, going left towards the river and Burneside Weir, over
a stile and across the field, following the River Kent upstream
before reaching the riverside beyond the next stile.

The river here is a deep and slow "Wind in the Willows" river,
its banks lined with reeds and tiny vole-holes. This is another
good area for birdlife, with mallard and swans usually to be seen,
with often impressive reflections in the slower moving waters.

The path is easy to find, over a ladder stile and along the riverside
to a second stile to Bowston Bridge. Cross the bridge (SD 499967),
to join the narrow lane from Burneside. Turn right here.

Continue along the road until just past the telephone box, look
for the narrow path on the right, signed Dales Way and Staveley,
passing between houses which takes the Dales Way back to the
riverside opposite the weir. There used to be another paper mill
here – its settling ponds are still to be seen, as is the line of a long
vanished light railway, once linking Burneside and Cowen Head
mills with the Windermere branch railway, and which now forms
part of the track used by the Dales Way. Continue along this little
access road to Cowen Head – another mill hamlet. Pass by
cottages, keeping right by the telephone kiosk and another weir
on this once very hard working, fast flowing river, to go through
a gate to join a pleasant riverside path.

Continue past Hagg Foot bridge and a lovely old barn, the
Dales Way now winding its way over a stile into and through
Cockshott Woods. Cross the next field; the next wall with a stile
is the Lake District National Park boundary – don't go through
the more obvious wall opening but veer left to locate a stile. This

stretch of riverside path now makes its way over narrow and awkwardly sloping, slate stones – hands are sometimes needed – but the attractive views and wooded areas more than compensate for the tricky features of the path. Soon past the trees the path once again becomes a level path, through narrow fields, before joining the main road at Sandy Hill, just south of the village of Staveley, now mercifully by-passed by the A591 and free of its incessant traffic.

Though not a main tourist centre, Staveley has an unusual clock tower, pleasant shops, an inn and cafe and both a railway station on the single track Windermere branch as well as a good bus service.

Take the signposted track, left, at Stock Bridge just before entering Staveley, indicating the Dales Way which goes past and around the 17th century Stock Bridge Farm (SD 474977) along a walled lane leading underneath the railway line. From here take the right of two tracks which, at the field end turns left along a wall to Moss Side Farm, crossing a stile in front of the buildings and along the drive to join the Crook road out of Staveley. Follow this road over the new by-pass, climbing up the lane to where a drive bears off right (SD 467976) towards Field Close. At the top of this, go left through a gate, then up the field to a kissing gate. The path climbs around the outside of a wood, climbing steadily, but you are rewarded with ever more impressive views of the circling fells. Continue to where the path joins an unfenced lane at a gate opposite New Hall farm.

Turn right here, following the lane as it climbs a low hill ahead, before descending to a junction with a broader tarmac lane near Waingap (SD 454963). Turn right here for 400 metres past Fell Plain Farm, now climbing to another junction by Glen Farm (SD 449966), where the Dales Way forks left along a green bridle-way. Where this enclosed track ends, go through the gate on the right (with waymarks) in the pasture alongside, and continue in the same direction along a faint green way, through typical Lakeland scenery with spikey crags puncturing the soft green pasture. Continue in roughly the same direction, but move slightly away from the wall on the left towards a gate, beyond which a clearer track is evident. This curves around to the right towards the edge of a small larch plantation. Keep ahead alongside (but do not cross) a small stream down to a gate. From here is a path through gorse which follows a wall on the right to join a track, by a barn, which leads to Crag House Farm (SD 435966).

Before the farm, turn right off this track which runs between a crag and the wall, ascending to a gate. Follow the wall on the right to a gate in the wall corner, passing some trees to reach a kissing gate at the bottom of the next field and a quiet farm road leading to Outrun Nook, a small group of farm buildings (SD 435968).

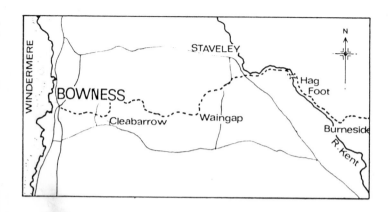

Continue along the lane for another 150 metres before bearing left along the access track to Hag End Farm (SD 439970). From Hag End the path goes past the farm buildings and through the yard, continuing along the line of the remains of a wall ahead, gradually ascending across rough grazing, and through a gap in another fallen wall. Keep ahead through a saddle or shallow pass in the hills, the summit on the right is Grandsire (818 metres).

At the top of the saddle (SD 427971)is a glorious moment when a great panorama of Lakeland fells opens out around you. Peaks to be seen if the weather is clear include Black Combe away to the west, the Coniston Fells, Crinkle Crags, Bowfell, Scafell in the distance, Langdale Pikes, Red Screes, Stony Cove Pike and the Kentmere Fells. In front is the great chasm between the fells that contains Windermere, a whole host of fir and pine covered knolls that make the Lakes District unique in England. This is the perfect place for a final pause before tackling the last part of the Dales Way.

The grassy path winds easily downwards by School Knoll, bearing left to a gate in the wall corner; turn left to a second gate to join a track crossed by a stream; follow the track left, and downhill as it becomes metalled and descends to join the busy B5284 Crook-Bowness road near Cleabarrow (SD 423962).

Turn right, and keep to the right hand side to face fast moving traffic along this road for 100 metres where a track bears right to Low Cleabarrow. Turn left before the farm buildings, go through a little gate on the left to descend along the path through two kissing gates, before ascending a field and past mature trees – follow the helpful waymarks – to the next gate in the wall. Keep ahead up another kissing gate, this time leading into a quiet lane close to Matson Ground (SD 417967).

Cross the road to another kissing gate, bearing left in the next field past Home Farm, kissing gates and waymarks making the path easy to follow. Keep in the same direction, through more gates, to a path by trees to another estate drive. Follow it for a few metres, then take the waymarked path ascending a path by young oaktrees and a metalled fence. Another metal gate at the top of the field leads through a short enclosed section of track to cross the access road to Brant Fell Farm (SD 409965), with the summit of Brant Fell itself looming directly behind the farm.

Continue in the same direction through another gate, before bearing right down the right hand edge of the next field to an open pasture on the brow of the hill, where for the first time Windermere itself – the lake and not the town – comes into view, over the rooftops of Bowness, its dark waters usually dotted with white sails.

The Dales Way continues to what is perhaps its real endpoint, a slate Lakeland seat erected by the South Lakeland Tourist Association and the National Trust (who own Brant Fell) dedicated "For those who walk the Dales Way". Enjoy the seat and the glorious view.

The path continues steeply down, through a kissing gate and into Brantfell Road. Ahead is Bowness, underneath its veneer of a tourist destination an intriguing village of narrow lanes and old inns, its medieval Parish Church of St. Martin's notable for a magnificent East window filled with 14th and 15th century glass, and an unusual 300-year-old carved figure of the legendary St. Martin who shared his cloak with a beggar.

Bowness has a far older history than the modern town and resort of Windermere, which until the mid 19th century was really two tiny Westmorland villages called Applethwaite and Birthwaite, which only became combined and known as Windermere when the railway station was opened in the 1840s, the railway company naturally wanting to attract excursionists with the name Windermere rather than that of these obscure villages. Not that this single track branch railway to Kendal and Oxenholme was without its opponents – no less a figure than William Wordsworth objected to the coming of the railway and its irresponsible hordes of visitors in letters to the newspapers and a somewhat unmemorable sonnet on the subject. Fortunately for Dales Way walkers, he wasn't successful.

Bowness has every facility a Dales Way walker could wish – a huge choice of accommodation from luxury hotels to simple bed and breakfast accommodation, and much in between, though be warned, the nearest Youth Hostel at Troutbeck is some distance away (open top buses to Ambleside go close by). Cafes, shops, pubs offer refreshment, whilst the Lake District National Park Visitor Centre offers detailed information about the area. There's even a fascinating steamboat museum down by the Lakeside, and a ferry over to Hawkshead.

A frequent Cumberland Motor Services shuttle bus service from the centre of Bowness links the town with Windermere Railway Station and with other parts of the Lake District.

Before leaving Bowness, there may be time to ignore the crowds strolling along the tiny promenade and make for Cockshot Point, a headland just beyond the end of the promenade. Here the fine expanse of England's largest lake and the background of mountains provide a grandeur and beauty recalling all 84 miles of dales, fells, moorland, crags, pasture and riverside which have been your companions for several days. Tired Dales Wayfarers have been known to dip hot and sweaty feet into its icy waters.

To complete the Dales Way is in itself no mean achievement in this soft and physically pampered age. It will be an experience that you will never forget.

THE NORTH'S LEADING PUBLISHER
FOR MORE THAN 40 YEARS

Here is a selection of other books which may interest you:

COMPLETE DALES WALKER VOL I: NORTHERN DALES
(ISBN 1 85568 070 X)

COMPLETE DALES WALKER VOL II: SOUTHERN DALES
(ISBN 1 85568 071 8)

COMPLETE LAKELAND WALKER
(ISBN 1 85568 053 X)

YORKSHIRE DALES STONEWALLER
(ISBN 1 85568 049 1)

A WALK THROUGH THE YORKSHIRE DALES
(ISBN 1 85568 047 5)

CUMBRIA WAY
(ISBN 0 85206 908 1)

With over 150 books to choose from the Dalesman range
covers subjects as diverse as:

WALKING, WILDLIFE, HUMOUR, TOPOGRAPHY
ANTHOLOGIES, HOLIDAY GUIDES, GHOSTS and SPORT

For a catalogue of all the Dalesman titles send a SAE to:

DALESMAN PUBLISHING CO LTD
CLAPHAM, VIA LANCASTER, LA2 8EB